Managing Your Software Project

Springer
London
Berlin
Heidelberg
New York
Barcelona
Budapest
Hong Kong
Milan
Paris
Santa Clara
Singapore
Tokyo

Ian Ricketts

Managing Your Software Project

A Student's Guide

Springer

Ian Ricketts, BSc, PhD
Department of Mathematics and Computer Science, The MicroCentre,
The University, Dundee DD1 4HN

ISBN 3-540-76046-6 Springer-Verlag Berlin Heidelberg New York

British Library Cataloguing in Publication Data
Ricketts, Ian W.
  Managing your software project : a student's guide
  1.Computer software - Development   2.Computer programming management
  I.Title
  005.1
ISBN 3540760466

Library of Congress Cataloging-in-Publication Data
Ricketts, Ian, 1951-
  Managing your software project : a students guide / Ian Ricketts.
  p.   cm.
  Includes bibliographical references and index.
  ISBN 3-540-76046-6
  1. Computer software- -Development- -Management.   2. Software
  engineering- -Management.   I. Title.
  QA76.76.D47R54   1997   97-34671
  005.1'078- -dc21   CIP

© Springer-Verlag London Limited 1998
Printed in Great Britain

Typesetting: Camera ready by author
Printed and bound at the Athenæum Press Ltd., Gateshead, Tyne and Wear
34/3830-543210 Printed on acid-free paper

Trademarks

Equation Editor is a special version of the *MathType* equation editor produced by Design Science Inc.

IBM and **PC-DOS** are registered trademarks of International Business Machines Corporation.

Microsoft is a US registered trademark and **MS-DOS**, **Windows**(tm) and **WORD** are trademarks of Microsoft Corporation.

Turbo C and **Turbo Pascal** are trademarks of Borland International.

Symantec C++ is a trademark of the Symantec Corporation.

Preface

About this Book

I wrote this book to help students who are about to start their first project. It provides guidance on how to organise your work so that you achieve your agreed objective.

The advice is based on experience gained from supervising more than 50 successful student projects, in both engineering and computer science, during the last 10 years. Projects have varied in duration from 120 hour final year undergraduate projects, through 800 hour MSc projects and up to 5000 hour PhD student research projects.

It is my experience that almost all students have the technical background, to a greater or lesser extent, to complete their assigned project but that a disappointingly large number lack the basic organisational framework. Once they are introduced to the rudiments of project management then they are better equipped to control their own progress. They can also concentrate their efforts more effectively on the technical challenges which they will inevitably meet. Of course you can improve your skills solely on the basis of personal experience but you are more likely to achieve your objectives, in a timely manner, with the help of an experienced guide. That is what I have tried to include within this book. It contains advice on how to solve some of the organisational challenges common to all projects so that you can successfully complete your project.

The guidance may also be of help if you are a relatively new supervisor of student projects or if you are looking for ideas on alternative approaches to supervision.

The underlying philosophy is that when a student is in control of their project then they are more likely to deliver their best work.

I hope this book will contribute towards that goal.

About the Author

Ian Ricketts obtained a joint honours degree (2.1) in Electrical Engineering and Economics from the University of Dundee in 1973 followed by a PhD in computing in 1977. He then joined Reuters on Fleet St, London working ultimately as a systems programmer on their share price reporting system before moving to NCR (Dundee) Ltd where he became project leader responsible for software development of their 24-hour banking terminal.

In 1980 he re-joined the University of Dundee as a lecturer with the Department of Electrical Engineering and Electronics. He subsequently joined the Department of Mathematics & Computer Science and is currently a Reader & Head of Undergraduate Studies in the Department of Applied Computing.

Dr Ricketts' research interests are in the application of computers to help people. He is the author/co-author of more than 100 journal and conference papers and joint holder of several software licences and patents adopted by UK and USA companies. He has supervised over 50 student projects and secured more than £1.8M in research funding.

Currently he jointly manages research assistants on a number of projects including software development for a European predictive word processing system, software to enhance basic numeracy, the application of computer based decision support to improve the management of patients with asthma, the development of software to support the efficient collection and analysis of information in community dentistry, a printing system for European users of sign language and providing access to computer based learning systems for users with disabilities.

Acknowledgements

There are a very large number of people who contributed to this book and though I will name but a few, I gratefully acknowledge the foundation provided by them all.

To Beverley and the team at Springer-Verlag for the encouragement and support.

To my teachers, both formal and otherwise, whose classes I have ceased to attend yet who still influence my actions, my thanks and my apologies for not paying more attention.

To the students and staff of the Department of Applied Computing at the University of Dundee, who provided many of the experiences on which this book is based and much of the fun that went with it.

To my Mother, Father, James and Andrea, I hope you are happy with the results.

To my wife Nora, who is largely responsible for my enjoyment of the last 25 short years and to Ben and Joan, who I fondly refer to as my children though they are no longer children, thanks for your love.

Finally, to you the reader, I acknowledge that as sole author I am responsible for all the errors and omissions that I know this book must contain despite my best efforts. I hope they do not distract you from successfully managing your project.

Contents

1. Introduction

The function of the menu outside a restaurant
is to encourage you to enter.
But the decision is all yours.

A Profile of the Expected Reader

I had the following reader in mind when I wrote this book:

1. You are a student who is about to embark on a software development project.

2. You have an experienced project supervisor who can advise you on how to conduct most aspects of your project but you would like to take this opportunity to get involved in the management of your project and do some reading ahead.

3. You have some experience of software development but little or no experience of project management and you want to change that.

4. You have a set of project guidelines, issued by your department, which say how to proceed but you also have some unanswered questions.

5. You are prepared to invest 2-3 hours reading what this author has to say and you will then integrate any new information with your supervisor's advice and your departmental guidelines to help you to produce a more successful project.

If the above profile is a reasonably good fit then you should find this book relevant and useful, otherwise you may wish to consider looking a little further along the bookshelf for a better match to your needs.

A Profile of this Book's Contents

This book contains six chapters in addition to this introduction. Each chapter should take no more than 30 minutes to read and I hope will repay your investment. The advice each chapter contains is intended to provide you with a framework around which you can build your project. As with all advice, question it in the light of your own experience and combine what you find helpful with the best advice of others to provide you with your project foundation.

In chapter two we explore how to create a plan for your project. The initial example is based on a single cycle of software development which we then refine to a 2-stage process. The intention is not that you will assume that all projects are 2-stage processes but that in the absence of other advice you will start with that and be comfortable assembling your own plan based on it. The chapter includes an example of a project plan produced using Microsoft Project.

In chapter three several topics are introduced under the collective title of Project Skills. These include encouraging you to use a single project handbook to hold all written information on the project, how to make the optimum use of your supervisor's limited effort, how to set about publishing those aspects of your project which will be of interest to others, how to cope with oral examinations, and finally how to cope with stress. It may seem premature to introduce these topics but I believe that in a successful project you need to consider them from the start of the project. More generally, I believe that solving the technical challenges is only one (minor) component of producing a successful solution.

In chapter four we examine how to collate your research data base. This involves contacting other researchers and seeking their assistance, using the library services and exploring the resources offered via the Internet, including Electronic Mail (Email), searching the World Wide Web (WWW), getting in touch with experts via News Groups and downloading the work of fellow researchers from some of the software and data archives.

In chapter five we focus on the tools available for report production. This includes encouraging you to apply effort to learning to touch-type. We examine the typical range of tools available with current word processors with examples using Microsoft Word for outlining, producing tables of contents and indexing. We also explore producing graphs, charts, drawings and the inclusion of mathematical equations. At the completion of this chapter you should have a sound appreciation of what is available to help you assemble and illustrate your project report.

In chapter six we focus on what is involved in writing your report. This includes a possible structure for the chapters and appendices plus strategies to assist you in improving your writing skills whilst producing the text for your chapters.

Finally in chapter seven we examine each phase of the software development process from creating the statement of requirements, through rapid prototyping to confirm the requirements specification, detailed design, design reviews, coding, verification and validation of the products of each stage including the various aspects of testing from the module level through to user acceptance.

The Three Functions of Management

Management, at its simplest, consists of a continuous cycle of three activities: Planning, Execution and Monitoring. Planning, which is examined in detail in the next chapter, is deciding what you will do and how long you will spend doing it. Execution is implementing the plan. Monitoring involves checking the execution to ensure that everything goes as planned and when deviations are detected then revising the plan so that the overall objectives are still met.

Executing a plan, at its simplest, is like following a familiar recipe. You are the chef. You have all the ingredients, the utensils are all available, and everything happens as described in the detailed instructions. You produce the dish on time and it is of an acceptable quality.

That is what happens when you execute an ideal project plan. Now imagine that you are required to plan a meal comprised of unfamiliar ingredients, e.g. whole pig, breadfruit and yams, requiring the use of cooking implements of which you have no previous experience, e.g. an open fire of driftwood and clay pots. You are also expected to follow the recipe and prepare a meal for 30 guests who will arrive, plate in hand, in 24 hours. Now that is more like the challenge of managing a software project.

I hope the information that you will find in the following chapters will equip you to deal with the inevitable challenges that you will meet whilst managing your software project.

2. Creating a Plan

Planning - a clean sheet of paper and anything is possible.

A project is largely predictable and therefore capable of being controlled. It consists of several standard activities which are performed sequentially. You can estimate the resources required to complete each activity and thereby plan for a project. This is what an experienced project manager can do and that is what you will be when you have completed your student project.

In this chapter you will be introduced to the activities within a software project, and shown how to estimate the effort needed to complete each activity and so arrive at a solution to the problem. This proposed solution is summarised in the Project Plan.

Identifying the Activities in a Software Project

The following table contains the activities defined by the classic 'Waterfall Model' [Schach93] of a software development project, together with the documents which are produced during each activity.

	Activity	Document
1.	(start)	Statement of Requirements
2.	Requirements Analysis	Requirement Specification
3.	Design	Design Specification
4.	Implementation	Implementation Specification
5.	Testing	Test Specification Test Reports
6.	(Operation & Maintenance)	User Manual

The delivery and acceptance (by the supervisor) of a document indicates that a phase of the project is complete. Delivery and acceptance of documents are useful milestones which you can use to monitor the progress of your project.

Estimating the Development Effort Required for Each Phase

A project history is a record of what actually happened in a project. It includes the effort actually expended on the various development activities. Once a number of project histories have been accumulated you can combine the results from several similar projects and produce an estimate for the next project.

Confidence in estimates based on accumulated project histories must be tempered with the knowledge that no two software projects are identical and that the seemingly small differences in two projects' requirements may result in significantly different divisions of project effort. In the absence of access to the histories of earlier and similar projects, take as your initial estimates the divisions of project effort as given in figure 2.1.

Remember that they are only estimates and that actual effort expended will need to be carefully monitored. Significant deviations from the plan will require you to modify the effort applied to later activities if the end point is to be achieved by the planned date, i.e. delivery of a completed project report.

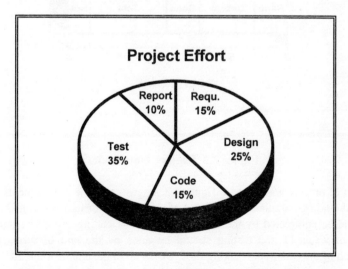

Figure 2.1 The Division of Effort Between Project Activities

I suggest you start with the divisions given in figure 2.1 and then make any adjustments which seem appropriate after discussion with your project supervisor.

Next you must agree with your supervisor the start and end dates for your project. Since you are the sole software developer on the project, the difference between these two dates will give you the maximum amount of effort (person-weeks) available to apply to the project. Should you not be available to work full-time on the project, say because there are lectures occupying each morning, then you must reduce the effort available proportionately.

Project Time Scale

Let us assume that you are to complete your project in 20 weeks and that you are available to work full-time on your project (i.e. 20 person-weeks of effort). Then if we use the divisions of effort as suggested in figure 2.1 the initial project time scale will be:

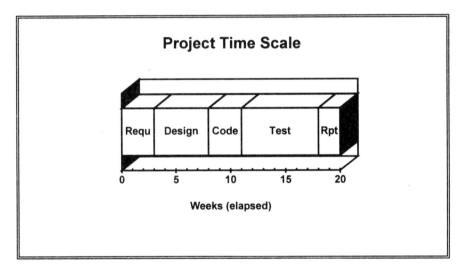

Figure 2.2 Project Time Scale

The chart of project time scale in figure 2.2 suggests that the requirements analysis activity should be completed by the end of week 3. The design is planned to take 5 weeks and be completed by the end of week 8. The coding should be finished by the end of week 11 and testing should be done by the end of week 18, with production of the final report taking the 2 weeks up to the end of week 20.

Once you place numbers against each activity you have started to manage. You begin to think in a more focused way, 'Well there are only 3 weeks to perform the requirements analysis and document it! First I need to produce the Statement of

Requirements and that will take me 1 day for the first meeting and then 2 days to document, then ......'. You can now refine your plan, just as with a program design, by adding detail and you can also monitor your progress against the plan and consider how to cope with deviations from the plan.

Now you really are managing your project.

An Alternative Division of Project Effort

The plan, shown in figure 2.2, will not deliver a working solution until the end of week 18. That is 2 weeks before the end of your project and rather late to discover that while the project has gone according to plan, the result may not match what the customer wanted! You might wish to consider a 2-stage approach in which, as before, you first complete the requirements phase culminating in production of the requirements specification. Then you have 2 cycles of design-code-test-report. The first stage is shorter than the second as can be seen in figure 2.3:

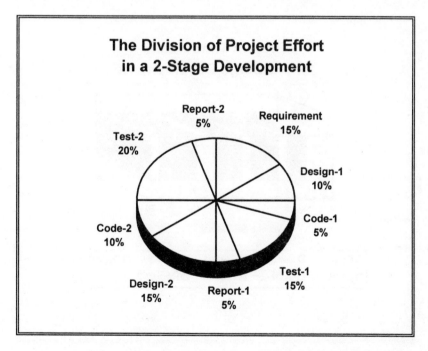

Figure 2.3 The Division of Project Effort in a 2-Stage Development

There are a number of advantages to the 2-stage approach:

- It provides an early opportunity to check the estimates in your plan.

- You create a prototype system for your customer to assess and comment on and you are still able to respond by making amendments in stage 2.

- Most importantly the 2-stage approach gives you the opportunity to learn from a brief experience of each phase of project solution while still allowing time for you to apply the lessons learned.

The Project Time Scale for a 2-Stage Development

Assuming the effort is applied over a 20-week period then an alternative view of the project time scale is given in figure 2.4.

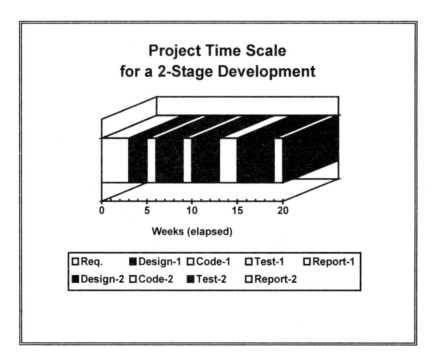

Figure 2.4 Project Time Scale for a 2-Stage Development

Translating the Effort into Production

Once you have agreed the start and finish date for the project and the number of persons working on the project, then you can calculate the size of the solution which can be produced. Having estimated the number of person-weeks of effort available you can translate that into person-days. I suggest you assume a maximum of 5 working-days per week and a maximum of 8 working-hours per day. Using these conservative figures will provide an in-built contingency which will help you to cope with unplanned activities and/or inaccurate estimates.

Estimating the Number of Lines of Source Code

You should be able to produce your commented computer program at a rate of 60 lines per day. That is assuming that you have already produced the detailed design and that testing and debugging are separate activities from coding. Assuming that we are planning for a 20-week full-time project, then according to the project time scale given in figure 2.4, coding will be completed in 3 person-weeks or 15 person-days. Therefore you will be able to produce a maximum of 900 lines of source code.

No module should be longer than a page, say 50 lines of source code. Thus the 900 lines of source code will be contained in a minimum of 18 separate modules.

Estimating the Effort to Create the Detailed Design

During the design phase, based on your knowledge of the problem as embodied in the requirements specification, you will produce a design for the system including an appropriate data structure. Typically the design will use a top-down approach and step-wise refinement. In the last refinement of the design, one statement of the design will be equivalent to one line of source code. The design process is explained later in the chapter on software development.

Assuming a 20-week project, the design phase would be allocated 5 person-weeks or 25 person-days of effort. You can assume that you will be able to produce a design at a rate of 40 lines per day so that you should be able to produce a maximum of 900 lines of design within the 25 days allocated.

Estimating the Effort to Write the Project Report

You can assume that you will write the report at a rate of 10 pages per day. This rate can be achieved because the production of the report is largely a task of assembling the information that has been already produced.

Thus for the 20-week full-time project, with an allocation of 2 weeks to report production, you would expect to be able to assemble a 100 page document.

Estimating the Effort to Test the Project Software

Software which contains even a small number of errors will be condemned as unreliable and not used. Testing and debugging are therefore very important and a significant proportion of your effort should be applied to them. I have recommended that 35% of the total project effort is allocated to the testing phase.

For the 20-week project this equates to 7 person-weeks of effort. Since there will be a minimum of 18 modules this means, that on average, you will have 2 days to test each module. In those 2 days you must define, document and perform the test and also debug any errors that are detected.

Identifying Deliverables and Milestones

Having estimated the time scales for each phase of your project your final step is to complete the development plan and to identify the deliverables associated with each phase. Deliverables on software projects are either completed software modules or completed documents.

Completed documents with their associated delivery dates make excellent project milestones since they can be readily checked for completion and are tangible, unlike software modules. Assuming a 2-stage development the project will have the following activities and associated deliverables:

Project Activities	Project Deliverables
	Statement of Requirements
Requirements Analysis	Requirement Specification
Stage 1	
Design	Design Specification for Stage 1
Implementation	Implementation Specification and Software Modules for Stage 1
Testing	Test Specification for Stage 1
	Test Reports for Stage 1
Reporting	Report for Stage 1
Stage 2	
Design	Design Specification for Stage 2
Implementation	Implementation Specification and Software Modules for Stage 2
Testing	Test Specification for Stage 2
	Test Reports for Stage 2
Reporting	Report for Stage 2
(Operation & Maintenance)	User Manual

Figure 2.5 Activities and Deliverables for a 2-Stage Project

Using the time scales suggested earlier you are now in a position to produce a draft project plan which includes the development activities, all deliverables and selected milestones. A draft plan for the 20-week project follows:

Project Activities		Milestones	
	Duration (week numbers)	Project Deliverables	Week ending number
	0	Statement of Requirements	0
Requirements Analysis	1-3	Requirement Specification	3
Stage 1			
Design	4-5	Design Specification Stage 1	5
Implementation	6	Implementation Specification and Software Modules for Stage 1	6
Testing	7-9	Test Specification for Stage 1	7
		Test Report for Stage 1	9
Reporting	10	Report for Stage 1	10
Stage 2			
Design	11-13	Design Specification Stage 2	13
Implementation	14-15	Implementation Specification and Software Modules for Stage 2	15
Testing	16-19	Test Specification for Stage 2	16
		Test Report for Stage 2	19
Reporting	20	Report for Stage 2	20
(Operation & Maintenance)		(User Manual)	

Figure 2.6 A Draft Plan for the 2-Stage 20-Week Project

Reviewing Your Project Plan

Discuss your draft project plan with your project supervisor, particularly the estimates for the levels of productivity in the various phases and the division of effort between the different phases. Consider carefully all suggestions made by your supervisor and modify your plan to reflect the results of your review.

A Tool for Maintaining Your Project Plan

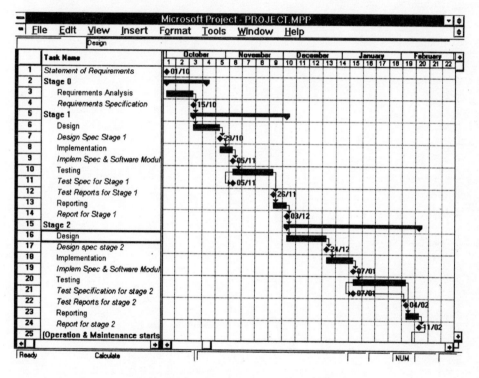

Figure 2.7 An Example of a Project Plan

Your project plan will form the basis of regular meetings with your supervisor when the deliverables and their due dates will be used to assess the project progress. Inevitably, some activities will not go exactly as planned and it will be necessary to modify the plan. Given that you expect to make changes, it is worthwhile considering using one of the many available software tools to help you with the task. Figure 2.7 is a 2-stage 20-week project plan. It was produced using Microsoft Project which is available on IBM compatible PCs.

All the above plans are based on the assumption that the 'Waterfall Model' is valid and there are many software engineers who would debate that view. However the important point is that you take a model, any model, and, in consultation with your supervisor, you adapt it to your needs. You then create a plan using it and agree dates for the various deliverables and then you manage your project using your plan. The aim is not to produce a perfect model but to produce a good model from which you can manage your (near) perfect project.

3. Gathering Your Project Skills

Preparation is an investment
which always yields a good return.

In the previous chapter you were introduced to the practical aspects of planning your software project. In this chapter we will explore the equally important components required to build a successful project, including keeping a project notebook, developing effective communications with your supervisor, publishing your project, preparing for oral examinations and coping with stress.

Keeping a Hardback Notebook

You will accumulate a lot of information during your project from a wide variety of sources. Get into the habit of writing it all in a hardback notebook. Use the notebook to record all information relating to your project including:

references	preliminary software designs
new ideas	contact names
draft meeting agenda	meeting reports
etc.	

Then when you need to retrieve an item you will know where to look and you will not have to start sifting through loose sheets of paper distributed around your various work sites.

Your Project Notebook will become a valuable article. Should you misplace it you can hasten its return by marking it clearly with:

Your Name
Departmental Address
Departmental Telephone Number

Include a folded self addressed envelope, large enough to take the handbook, inside the handbook's front cover, and include in bold print the notice that

A reward will be paid for the return of this book

Communicating with Your Supervisor

Your supervisor is a potentially important contributor to your project because he/she has a considerable reservoir of technical and organisational experience. The more you can involve them in your project the more likely it is that you will be able to combine their experience with your effort to achieve a satisfactory solution.

The problem is that your supervisor will also be involved, willingly or otherwise, in numerous other activities. These will occupy 95% of their time. Therefore, you need to make best use of the remaining 5% and to do that you need to keep your supervisor informed, interested and involved in project progress. Thus your communications with your supervisor need to be both effective and efficient.

Provide Regular Progress Reports

Your supervisor is short of time, so make their task easier - keep them up to date on your progress and plans by providing short written reports in advance of meetings and always include summaries. The information contained in your progress reports will form part of your final project report.

Organise Project Meetings

I suggest that initially you plan to have regular weekly meetings with your supervisor lasting no longer than 1 hour. Once the project is running according to your plan then you may agree to reduce the frequency of meetings to once a fortnight.

Start and finish all meetings promptly. If you are going to be delayed then let your supervisor know as soon as possible and agree to delay the start of the meeting or reschedule it. At the start of each meeting confirm the finishing time for the meeting and agree the agenda. A typical agenda might contain:

1. A report of the last meeting

2. Progress

3.   Plans

4.   Any Other Business (AOB)

5.   Date and time of the next meeting

The 'Report of the last meeting' is the obvious item with which to start each meeting. It serves to remind everyone as to the current status of the project and what was agreed at the last meeting. It consists of a summary of the items discussed and the actions agreed. You should produce this immediately after each meeting so that it is clear to both you and your supervisor what the outcomes of each meeting were. These reports can also be included in the appendix to your final report as evidence of your ability to successfully manage the project.

Under 'Progress' you report what was achieved with reference to the project plan. When you are reporting get into the habit of summarising. You might say, "This is the end of week 3 and the project work is proceeding as planned". If further detail is requested you might add, "the statement of requirements has been agreed and the first draft of the requirements specification has been completed". If still further detail is requested then you might add, "Preparation of the 2 page statement of requirements took 3 days. The draft requirements specification is now 15 pages in length and took 12 days to assemble including getting familiar with the word processor …".

Under 'Plans' you review what is to happen next and if necessary agree any modifications required to time scales caused, for example, by lack of access to equipment. By the end of this item on the agenda you will have either agreed that the current plan is accurate or you will have decided on modifications which you will incorporate into the revised plan immediately after the meeting.

Under 'AOB' you discuss those items not previously dealt with under Progress and Plans e.g. your supervisor would like you to provide a demonstration for a party of visitors, you've had difficulty finding an unoccupied computer because of the number of *game players* and want priority access, etc. Lastly you agree the date and time of the next meeting and the deliverables, if any, that will be ready for it.

Immediately after each meeting you produce a brief (1 page) report on the actions arising from the meeting, an updated project time scale and a list of the agreed deliverables for the next meeting. Make sure your supervisor receives a copy.

It is common for there to be more items for discussion on an agenda than time available. If it appears that you are not going to complete all the agenda items then agree priorities for the remaining items and if necessary agree maximum times for each item. Then follow your meeting plan. Carry forward to the next meeting's agenda any items not dealt with.

In the appendices to this book you will find examples of both an agenda and a report of a project meeting.

Maintaining Your Supervisor's Involvement

You should endeavour to maintain the interest of your supervisor in your project. You can do this by keeping them up to date on the technical developments via your technical reports, which they can re-use, and by involving them in the triumphs. In return you can expect to call on their considerable technical and managerial experience to help resolve any problems with your project.

Be clear what your objectives are, both for all meetings and for the project as a whole. Be clear also as to the objectives of your supervisor. Recognise that not all objectives will be shared. For example your primary objective is the production of the project report which will contribute to the grade of your degree. Your supervisor may have, as a primary objective, obtaining the solution to a research problem which is the subject of your project. The two objectives are similar but not identical. Ideally you should aim to achieve both and thereby ensure the support of your supervisor, but remember that solving the research problem is of secondary importance.

Assuming that you successfully manage your project, i.e. produce an acceptable project report by the due date, your next task will be to apply for jobs. Your project supervisor is an obvious choice for referee in support of your applications for employment i.e. someone willing to attest to your good character and technical abilities. First confirm that your supervisor is willing to act as a referee. Then provide a curriculum vitae (CV) so that your supervisor can more easily produce a reference. An example of a short CV is included in the appendix.

Publishing Your Project

Publishing your project is likely to be a shared objective since both student and supervisor gain credit from publications. This is an activity which is best embarked on after you have completed the first draft of your project report. By that stage you will have available all the information required and in a form that is most easily modified to that required for publication. It is extremely unusual to find a publisher willing to accept an unmodified project report.

Let us assume that you have just completed the Gold Price Prediction System used as an example in the appendix. For a summary read the Statement of Requirements.

Publications, in whatever form, start with you asking and answering 5 basic questions:

1. Where is the potential audience?
2. What is the best medium to reach the audience?
3. What knowledge does the reader have of the subject?
4. What information do I want to communicate?
5. Is there a standard format for delivery?

Where is the Potential Audience?

The findings of your Gold Price Prediction project could be of interest to dealers in stocks and shares, managers of pension funds, and researchers in artificial neural networks, to mention just a few. So you could contact your library or the appropriate professional body and identify what journals these people read. Then you could obtain copies of the journals. In the journals you will normally find *Guidance Notes for Authors* which you should read carefully and several examples of the style of article that the editors prefer to publish. You are looking for a journal which has a style with which you have some affinity. Do not be surprised if you have to discard several before you find a potential recipient for your publication.

Among the advertisements within the journals you will also find *Calls for Papers* from the organisers of forthcoming conferences. Perhaps one of these overlaps with your project area. If so then ask them for an *Author's Pack* which will describe in detail the format to which they require all contributing papers to conform.

What is the Best Medium to Reach the Audience?

The following is a list of possible media with the earlier entries being potentially easier (and quicker) routes to publication:

1. 1-day workshops
2. conferences
3. journals
4. books

Workshops tend to have shorter publication delays with potentially 3-9 months between the *Call for Papers* and the workshop being held and its proceedings published. Conferences, being larger affairs, have longer time scales, typically 9-18 months. Journals tend to take 12-24 months to publish an article and publishing delays with a book can be even longer.

I would suggest that you start with publishing at a local workshop and that you wait until your reputation has spread before offering to write your first book.

What Knowledge Does the Reader Have of the Subject?

To communicate effectively you must make an assessment of the likely expertise of your audience. It would be unwise to spend valuable time explaining the operation of an artificial neural network to an audience at the annual workshop on artificial neural networks and you would probably be equally unsuccessful if you assumed that background knowledge when addressing a meeting of pension fund managers. As with all things, seek the advice of your supervisor.

What Information Do I Want to Communicate?

Assuming that you have recently completed a 20-week project you will not be short of information to impart. The difficulty is to decide which information is most relevant to the particular audience. That will depend both on their background and on the stated aim of the workshop. For example, if the workshop was on 'recent applications of neural networks' then you would need to carefully explain the concept of gold price prediction before explaining your particular solution. However if the conference was aimed at 'share price predictions using neural networks' you would not expect to need to introduce either the topic of artificial neural nets or share price prediction but to concentrate on the original aspects of your method and its results.

Is There a Standard Format for Delivery?

The format for reporting work is surprisingly standardised whatever the medium used. The volume of information transmitted in a 20 page journal article will be considerably larger than that given in a 10 minute delivery at a workshop but the format will probably follow:

Summary

A very brief description of what you tried to do and how successful you were in doing it.

Introduction

This should contain an explanation of the problem that you set out to solve and why you chose it. It should also reference others who have worked on this or similar problems and with whom you may subsequently compare results.

Method

This contains a complete explanation of the approach or approaches taken to solve the problem. Assuming your work can withstand the comparison, it makes sense to include at least one competing approach reported elsewhere so that readers/listeners can understand why your work represents an advance on that previously performed.

Results

You should include sufficient data on the outcome of your work so that others can implement your method and confirm that your results are repeatable.

Discussion and Recommendations

This is where you give your interpretation of the results and with the benefit of hindsight suggest what you or others could do to improve on the performance given more time / equipment / modified methods / etc.

Writing a Conference Paper

The first step is to find a suitable conference and get a copy of its *Call for Papers*. Successful conferences are usually repeated at regular intervals e.g. annually, bi-annually, etc. and your supervisor will probably be able to suggest a shortlist. You will also find publicity for forthcoming conferences by consulting the appropriate Internet News Group (see chapter four).

Once you have located a suitable conference then use your library services to get a copy of past proceedings and read some of the articles, relevant to your field of interest, to confirm the style used in successful papers. You can also confirm any deviations from the standard format as described in the previous section.

Produce a draft submission based on the guidelines supplied in the *Call for Papers* and on examples you have read in earlier proceedings. Take care to follow all the editor's instructions, as any deviations may result in your submission being rejected without consideration of its technical merit.

Discuss the draft version with your supervisor and then, after making any agreed revisions, submit the final version to the conference editor in advance of the inevitable deadline.

Writing a Journal Paper

The approach is similar to that for a creating a conference paper. You first get copies of the journal and read relevant articles to confirm the preferred style for submissions. Then if the journal is an appropriate target for your proposed paper you must locate the *Authors' Notes* which you can obtain either from a recent copy of the journal or directly from the journal editor. The editor's name and address will be given in the journal.

Some journal editors ask you to provide an outline including title and abstract, so that they can confirm your article's relevance to the journal's readership prior to you committing yourself to producing the full text. Other editors prefer to receive a complete article. Read any instructions provided by the editor carefully and follow them exactly. Failure to follow instructions is a prime reason for submissions being rejected.

Produce your draft and discuss its content and format with your supervisor. Make any agreed revisions and then submit it to the journal's editor. You should receive confirmation that your submission has been received within a couple of weeks. You then have to wait for the feedback from the journal's reviewers which will take a further 6-12 weeks.

On receipt of the reviewers' comments make the requested revisions and return your updated article together with a letter detailing the revisions made. A successful format for your letter is to quote each comment made by the reviewers and to reply to it stating the changes you made. Do submit your revised article before the deadline otherwise your submission will be rejected and your effort wasted.

More articles are submitted than are published and the more experienced writers tend to have greater success than the less experienced. To be successful you will need to cope with the occasional rejection. When a journal rejects your article take a short break, while your pride repairs, then revise your article and submit it to a competing journal. As with many things, tenacity is a pre-requisite to achieving success.

Giving an Oral Presentation

Oral presentations take many forms. You may be required to give a talk to a group of academic staff visiting your department, or to present your work to a group of school children attending your University Open Day, or you may present your work at a national conference.

The approach is the same although the level of anxiety may vary. Just as with communicating any information you must identify the likely knowledge of the audience and assemble content accordingly. You need to identify the length of talk required and the appropriate medium for delivery. It is easier to deliver a talk using 35mm slides or computer projection, since you will probably not be able to see the audience, than to stand at a lectern and give a speech perhaps supported by acetate overheads.

You should be wary of using live demonstrations to support a presentation. This applies especially if you are in an unfamiliar location and using borrowed equipment. A demonstration can be spectacularly successful but similarly it can produce a memorable failure and you may not wish to risk exposing your audience to such extremes of emotion.

There are several software packages available to help you to produce material for presentations. I currently use Microsoft Powerpoint to create material destined for delivery as 35mm slides, acetate slides or direct computer projection. Alternatively you can assemble professional looking slides using the facilities of most word processors.

I would suggest the following guidelines when assembling the content for slides:

1. Pictures, simplified diagrams and graphs are more interesting than text

2. Use only machine printed text unless you are a graphic artist

3. Text only slides should have a maximum of 8 lines

4. Use a simple font e.g. Arial

5. Use the largest font compatible with (3) above

6. Use headings not sentences

7. Choose colours to maximise readability not to entertain

8. Plan to deliver slides at a maximum rate of 1 per minute

Structure your talk as if it was a paper but only put the outline plus the illustrations on the slides. You will deliver the details in your talk.

You need to take particular care to structure a talk so that the audience knows what is coming and what progress is being made in the overall delivery. A proven technique is to give the equivalent of a *table of contents* i.e. a single slide providing a summary of your talk in the form of its major headings, then as you deliver the talk you remind the audience where you are in the structure. Finally, at the end of the talk you remind the audience what headings you have covered.

Once you have assembled the contents of the slides you should create a script to accompany your slides. To do this assume that you are writing the talk for someone else to deliver. A typical script might look like:

Slide 1 (Title & Author)   start at 0 minutes

  Good evening ladies and Gentlemen,

  My name is Alan Turing and I would like to welcome you to the first meeting of the British Computer Society.

  Tonight I hope to give you an insight in to our research into a new field which we call Artificial Intelligence.

                              stop at 1 minute

Slide 2 (Contents)   start at 1 minute

  I will start this evening's talk by introducing the ....

The script should contain everything that the speaker will say and how long they should take to say it. You should then print the script on to postcards using 1 card per slide. The start and stop times for each slide should be clearly visible.

To deliver your presentation you then start your stop watch when you stand up and read the script. You adjust your rate of delivery to ensure that you complete the talk as per the schedule.

If you are preparing an important talk then practise your talk on a local audience and revise the content in the light of experience.

Finally, always check the equipment in advance of giving a talk and make sure you know which room you are using, ensure that there is suitable blackout available, that you know how to operate the projector, the light dimmer and the pointer.

Good preparation usually leads to a sparkling performance.

Making the Most of an Oral Examination

An oral examination or *viva voce* may form part of your final project assessment. The format will vary from department to department and your supervisor will confirm the exact style that you will meet. A common format is that you will meet with a panel of examiners, who may have already seen your written report, and they will ask you questions:

1. To confirm that you are the author of the report.

2. To clarify any points that the report did not make clear.

3. To assess the extent of your knowledge and understanding of the topic.

4. To explore areas which you may not have included in the report but which the examiners consider important.

Preparing for an Oral Examination

Confirm with your supervisor the start time, location and expected duration of the examination. Most examiners like to put the examinee at ease and start the session with a general question such as, "Give a brief summary of your project requirements and how you met them", so prepare a five minute summary of your project and practise delivering it without referring to notes.

In consultation with your supervisor compile a short list of example questions. Typical questions asked by examiners include:

> What relevant work did you locate by other researchers?

> What was the most challenging part of your project and how did you overcome it?

> What aspects of your project are novel?

> What part of your project gave you the most satisfaction and why?

> If you were to repeat your project what would you do differently?

Prepare one minute answers to each of the questions and be ready to deliver them without notes.

Some initially complex answers become readily understood when combined with a simple sketch. Identify the five or six sketches which will help you to communicate your project and practise delivering them.

Ask your supervisor to make a note of the questions, your answers and any further comments by the examiners. This will provide a framework for any revisions that you may wish to make to your report.

Finally, re-read your report before the oral examination but organise your preparation so that you complete it the day before the meeting. Take the evening off before the oral exam and get a full night's sleep.

At the Examination

Dress smartly for the examination. Assume that first impressions do count and make sure that they count in your favour. Arrive 5-10 minutes before the examination is due to commence. Being late for an examination will not provide you with a relaxed start and will not count in your favour.

Listen carefully to each question and ask for clarification if you do not understand what is being asked of you. The examination is not a race and the examiners are interested in the quality of your responses not the quantity. Take time to consider each question and your reply before answering. When answering a question, look at the questioner and speak clearly and slowly. Remember that you are an expert on your project and the examiners are interested in what you achieved, so be confident.

Keep your replies short (maximum 1 minute) and offer to expand on them if required. Be honest in your replies and if you do not know the answer to a question then say so. Consider using sketches to illustrate any points that you make or refer the examiners to drawings within your report but do not read from your report.

What to do After the Exam

Meet with your supervisor and on the basis of the notes taken at the oral examination consider what revisions, if any, you could usefully make to your report. Agree any changes and make them immediately after the meeting while your recollections are strongest.

Coping with Stress

Stress is that feeling you have when dealing with the unfamiliar (e.g. examinations, interviews, talking to a group) or situations in which you do not feel in full control e.g. travelling as a passenger in the front seat of a car. A similar feeling can arise when you are working on your project, especially when deadlines are approaching more quickly than expected.

Learning to cope with stress is part of the student experience. At least one employer that I know says "graduates are attractive as employees because they have demonstrated that they can cope with stressful situations and thrive".

Unfortunately every year a number of students find themselves temporarily incapable of continuing their studies because they are unable to cope with stress. The walking wounded seek support from their friends, supervisors and/or student counsellors. Some feel sufficiently ill that they seek the advice of their general medical practitioner. And tragically, each year, a number of students commit suicide as a direct result of failing to cope with stress.

In this section I suggest some simple strategies to keep you from becoming one of the walking wounded. If these strategies don't work for you but something else does then use it. However if you feel that nothing seems to work for you then call for help sooner rather than later. Almost every problem that a student faces has been met before and successfully resolved with a little help from a friend. Every University and College has staff specifically qualified to deal with the major problems and all staff are there to help you, so please do not suffer in silence.

Strategies for Coping with Stress

Consider preparing, well in advance, for a predictably stressful event. This requires an investment in effort but the 'return on investment' of being in control usually more than compensates. The obvious example is planning revision for exams so that you complete your revision at least the day before the exam rather than revising throughout the night before.

Learn from other people's experiences. It can be a lot less expensive than building up your own. Discuss your problems with your friends and ask them how they would deal with them. You do not have to be direct. Many of us use the "If you found yourself with ... how would you deal with it?". You'll probably have to reciprocate and contribute your experiences to help your advisers to deal with their own problems but that can expand your horizons as well.

Consider developing specific strategies to deal with potentially stressful situations. Try compiling a list of the 5 most stressful types of situation which you meet in the course of normal activity. Now consider how you might prepare yourself to deal with each one of them, e.g.

a)   if you lack the confidence to speak at a meeting - you might consider attending a short course on presentation skills, or joining a reading circle in which you will discuss people's writings, or joining a debating group, or just expressing more of your views in discussions with friends.

b) if you lack the confidence when writing reports you might consider an evening class in creative writing, etc.

Taking regular breaks in the form of exercise is one of the more powerful ways of coping with stress. While you are exercising you will not be thinking about work but rather "How did I get in to this wetsuit" or "Where is the service line in badminton", or "I wonder if my partner would like to share a pizza after this next dance".

All universities and colleges have extensive sports facilities and supporting organisations whose main function is to ensure that you, as a student, enjoy using the facilities. Sports Unions and Departments of Physical Education aim to provide a welcoming environment and introductory training courses plus introductions to other people who have similar skills to yours and want to take a break from work. Join a club and establish a circle of friends who have different interests and can therefore provide an alternative view of (or solution to) the challenges that you may meet. When you talk a problem over with a friend it is at least halved and sometimes resolved.

Beware of overworking. I recommend that in planning your work you assume a maximum of 40 working hours per week, preferably spent during the five week days thus leaving the weekend free for leisure. You should also plan your working day so that it contains approximately equal proportions of work, relaxation and sleep. Stop work at least 2 hours before going to bed and don't take your work to bed as reading material. You have given it eight hours already and you will need a fresh mind for tomorrow's eight hours.

Finally, at the risk of sounding like a parent, try to eat regularly and aim to maintain a reasonably balanced diet. Preparing food can be relaxing and has the added advantage of being cheaper than eating out or buying meals ready-made. Cooking food for friends can also be a very social activity. At your simplest you are a machine which needs fuel to function and good fuel to excel. In the same vein, beware of using alcohol as a regular relaxant. The recommended maximum weekly intake is 20 units for a man or 14 units for a woman. A unit is equivalent to half a pint of beer or a glass of wine. Drinking 3 pints of beer each night will damage your bank balance in the short term and probably your health in the longer term.

4. Collating Your Research Data Base

Being first is exhausting.
In a race it is much easier to run at the shoulder of the leader
until you can make your bid for the finishing tape.

Ignore the work of earlier projects at your peril since you risk repeating what has already been done, perhaps using methods which have already been identified as inferior and you thereby lose claim to your work making an original contribution. You will also be wasting your valuable resources.

A typical project contains a (small) element of original work plus a (much larger) foundation of previous work. The optimum approach is to identify the important contributions made by earlier workers and familiarise yourself with them. You should also identify who is currently active in the field and what their areas of activity are. You will then be in a good position to choose where to apply your own efforts, building on previous work.

The management decision that you have to make is what proportion of your overall effort you assign to your search. That is an important decision and worthy of discussion with your supervisor but, whatever you agree, the quantity and quality of the results of your research will depend on where you search and how you search.

This chapter will provide guidance on how and where to look for relevant information.

As you find new items of relevant information, make a note of their source i.e.

Title:

Author(s):

then if it was a book:

ISBN:

Publisher:

Date:

or if is was a journal paper:

Journal Title:

Publication Date:

Volume Number:

Article Page Numbers:

or if it was a project report:

Awarding Institution:

Submission Date:

and include a brief summary of the content plus your assessment of its strengths and weaknesses.

The information that you gather and your assessment of its contribution to the solution represents a significant piece of work and will form the basis of another section of your project report.

Talking to Other Researchers

Ask your supervisor to suggest who you should talk to within your department or faculty. Remember when you do contact people that you are asking them to give their time which is their most precious resource.

First impressions do count. It's a good idea to start by asking if they are free to talk to you and then ask to make an appointment. Tell them who you are, what you are doing and what you hope to achieve by meeting with them. Suggest how long the meeting will last. Finally agree a date and time.

The more professional you are, the more likely it is that you'll get your meeting. The clearer you are about the aims of the meeting the more likely it is that the meeting will be productive.

If you make your initial contact by memo it might look something like the following:

> *Hello Ms Smith,*
>
> <u>*Rule-Based Systems Applied to Checking the Spelling of English Sentences*</u>
>
> *My name is Helm Holtz and I am a 4th year student in Applied Computing. I am currently starting my project on the design and implementation of an English language spelling checker under the supervision of Dr Charlotte Bronte. I understand that you have experience in rule-based systems and may be willing to advise me as to their application to this problem. I am particularly interested to hear of any similar work and your suggestions as to background reading. If you could spare 20 minutes of your time to help me I would be most grateful.*
>
> *I am available to meet with you at your office on any afternoon this next week and I can be contacted at helmholtz@computing.dundee.ac.uk via the electronic mail system or c/o The Departmental Office of Applied Computing.*
>
> *Thank you,*
>
> *Helm Holtz.*

Once you establish a meeting there are a number of additional questions which you can ask of a willing adviser:

Recommended Reading

Your adviser may be able to assess your level of understanding of the topic and suggest suitable sources of information to bridge the gap between what you know and what you need to know. Given the limited resources available in most libraries the adviser may also be willing to lend you their copies.

Specifically you should ask for their recommendations as to what sources of information are locally available and particularly can they suggest:

> a 'best' book
>
> a 'best' project report

a 'best' journal(s)

for you to consult. Take great care of their property and return it promptly, otherwise you will find your pool of expert advisers will evaporate very quickly.

Very soon your problem will not be one of too little information but of too much.

Accessing Library Services

Every college has an expert team of information researchers and almost all of them are to be found behind the counter of your library. Using your professional approach you will quickly be able to enlist their support to locate material relevant to your needs.

If you are not already familiar with the research services available at your library then ask for an introductory tour. Find out what relevant textbooks are available for loan and which are only available for consultation within the library. Find out where the project reports are held and examine the last 5 years for relevant material. Search the journal section for relevant material.

Keep a note of useful titles and their locations so that you can re-examine them later.

Getting Familiar with Your Local Libraries

The college library is not the only source of information. There may be libraries attached to departments other than your own which have relevant material. There will also be the local council reference or main library and there are probably reciprocal arrangements between your own college and neighbouring college libraries so a visit to them may be justified.

As you will quickly appreciate, gathering information is time consuming and you will need to plan carefully what proportion of your time you can allocate to this activity. You should plan to complete the bulk of your background research during the requirements and design phases but you should never stop looking for information. The amount of effort you assign to this activity will depend both on the length and type of project and should be a topic for careful discussion with your supervisor.

Finding and Reading the Reports of Remote Researchers

You can locate a report by a remote researcher in a number of different ways:

(i) You may find a **Reference to it in a paper** that you already have in your local library

(ii) You may find a reference to it in an **Abstract Journal** which is compiled using abstracts from reports published say in the last 3 months.

(iii) You may find it cited in a **Citation Index** which lists, for a particular set of recently published papers, all authors/papers which have the cited paper in their list of references.

You can use an Abstract Journal to locate a paper, then use the references in the paper to locate earlier related work and use a Citation Index to locate later related work. Once you have found an author who is reporting work of interest you can search abstract journals under that author's name.

Abstract Journals and Citation Indices are held in most main libraries but unfortunately each request from your library for a loan from a remote library, called an Inter Library Loan, costs approximately £5. Increasingly institutions are asking readers to pay that cost when they make the loan request. Consequently you may find your use of the Inter Library Loan service curtailed!

There is however a potential solution to these Inter Library Loan charges and that is to gather your information via the Internet.

Gathering Information via Computer Networks

Almost all universities and colleges have their computers interconnected. A network of computers enables users, say in the Department of Biology, to access the journal index held on the main library computer and having identified a reference to an interesting article, to print that reference on the printer in the Dept of Biology. All this is achieved without the user moving from their chair!

In the UK the individual campus networks are all interconnected so that a registered user at Bristol University can search the library index at the University of Dundee as easily as searching their local library. Using the same network, registered users can exchange electronic mail messages or transfer copies of software or reports. The UK network also includes access to many company networks making the exchange of information between researchers in academia and those in companies that much easier. Potentially all registered users on a network can share information and national networks like this exist in Europe, USA, Australia and most of the developed countries, and almost all of them are interconnected.

Access to these electronic networks is currently free of charge for teaching and research users and via them it is possible to reach the corners of the globe, often within minutes.

To find out about the wide range of facilities available you should contact the people responsible for information technology services in your college and ask about local access to the Internet.

Electronic Mail (Email)

One of the simplest and most useful facilities available via the Internet is access to electronic mail. The Information Technology Service within your college will issue you with an electronic mail address, e.g. ricketts@dundee.ac.uk, which can be read as user ricketts whose electronic mail box is in Dundee which is an academic institution in the UK. Your Information Technology Service will also provide access to a suitable mail-tool to enable you to exchange electronic messages.

Your email box address is unique. A user with access to the Internet anywhere in the world can send electronic mail messages to your mailbox provided they know your email box address. Receipt of messages sent from across the other side of the world takes only a matter of minutes and when you next execute your mail-tool you will be notified of the arrival of any new messages and you can then reply to the sender, or forward the email to other users, or place the message on hold until you have an opportunity to deal with it.

One example of a mail-tool, available on IBM compatible Personal Computers, is Microsoft's Internet Mail. Once the Internet mail-tool is loaded, you select the *New Message* Icon to get help to create your email message.

You are then presented with a pre-formatted memo in to which you have to enter 3 pieces of information: the address of the destination mailbox i.e. "Colin McCowan", the subject of the email i.e. "Re: Trials of the Asthma Software" and finally the body of the email i.e. "Hi Colin ....". The completed email is shown in Figure 4.1. Once you are satisfied with the content of the email you click on the *Send* icon which is cunningly disguised as an envelope.

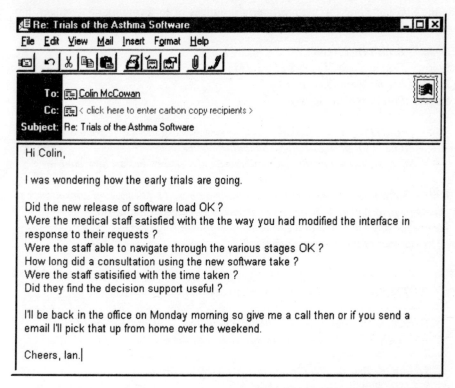

Figure 4.1 An Example of Electronic Mail Using Microsoft's Internet Mail

The functions offered by a mail-tool are rather more extensive than just creating and sending emails. Most mail-tools include facilities for maintaining an address book, sending single emails to multiple destinations, storing and retrieving emails, attaching documents to emails, encryption and much more. However the basic functions and interfaces are largely common across the various mail-tools so that once you are familiar with one mail-tool you should experience little difficulty transferring to another.

List Servers & Special Interest Groups (SIGs)

A List Server is a source of emails related to specific topics. Once you have an electronic mail box you can choose to register your email box address with one or more of the many List Servers which are associated with Special Interest Groups (SIGs - pronounced like 'pigs' but with an 's').

They provide newsletters and postings to registered members on topics of interest to the SIG including discussions/tutorials, notices of forthcoming conferences, job opportunities and book reviews, e.g.

From: British HCI News
Sent: Friday, June 27, 1997 11:53 AM
To: bcs-hci@mailbase.ac.uk
Subject: Post at Whizzo Software

~~~~~   *BRITISH HCI GROUP :: http://www.bcs.org.uk/hci/ :: NEWS SERVICE*
~~~~~*All news to: bcs-hci-request@mailbase.ac.uk ~~~~~~~~~*
~~~~ *News archives: http://www.mailbase.ac.uk/lists/bcs-hci/archive.html* ~~~~

Whizzo Software provides scientific/engineering based software and consultancy to clients in government, industry and commerce throughout the world.
We are looking for bright and enthusiastic Software Engineers ...
... (remainder of this message removed)

~~~~~~~~~~~
    NOTE: Please reply to article's originator, not the News Service
~~~~~~~~~~

    To receive HCI news, send mailbase@mailbase.ac.uk the message:
        JOIN BCS-HCI your_firstname your_lastname
~~~~~~~~~

    To join the British HCI Group, contact hci@bcs.org.uk
    Info: http://www.bcs.org.uk/hci/
~~~~~~~~~~

Each List Server has an associated email address and to register you normally send an email message to the List Server including the word 'Join' in the body of the email. The typical List Server will respond, within minutes, with an email message confirming that you are now registered, instructions on how to de-register, an explanation of the aims of the associated SIG and where to send any information that you wish to be included in a posting. The volume of information that you receive depends entirely on the size, and more importantly the activity levels, of the membership of the SIG.

At best, List Servers can provide a rich source of current information compiled by international experts in the field and delivered at no cost to your email in-tray. Conversely, a List Server can provide a seemingly endless stream of emails which threaten to fill your electronic in-tray with items of little or no interest and which will take the remainder of your day to delete. The solution is simple. Once the information is no longer welcome you remove yourself from the List Server. You can always rejoin later.

World Wide Web (WWW)

The World Wide Web (WWW) is an alternative view of the information available on the Internet. You can create a Web Page, containing information that you wish to share, using *Microsoft Front Page* or a similar program. You then make your Web Page accessible to other Internet users by linking your Web Page to a Web Server.

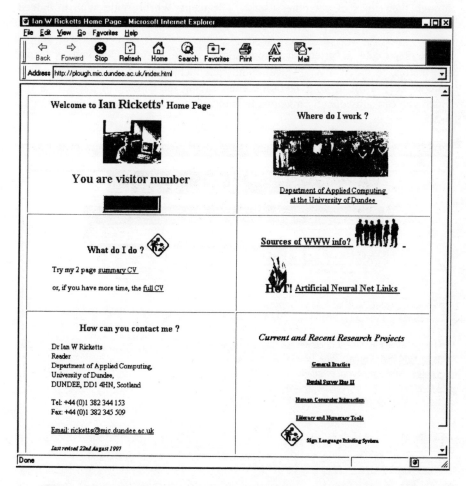

Figure 4.2 Using Microsoft's Internet Explorer to Browse the WWW

You will need Web Browser software to access the WWW. Two popular examples of Web Browsers available for IBM and compatible PCs are Netscape and Microsoft Internet Explorer. Figure 4.2 shows Microsoft's Internet Explorer being used to browse a WWW page. Consult your college's Information Technology

Service for advice on which browser they support and whether they offer an introduction to its use.

The term Web Page refers to the way you view the content one page at a time. When the information extends to more than a single page you create your Web Pages with visible links to connect the pages together. Subsequently when a user is browsing through your pages and selects a link, perhaps shown as underlined text, they will be transferred immediately to a view of the linked page. The richness of the WWW becomes apparent when you include links to other people's pages and through their links to yet other users. The name World Wide Web is indeed appropriate.

Browsers provide a variety of commands to make it easier for you to locate information on the WWW. Typical commands include an address book in which you can keep a list of your favourite sites, saving the content of pages in a file which you can subsequently manipulate with your word processor or transmit in an email.

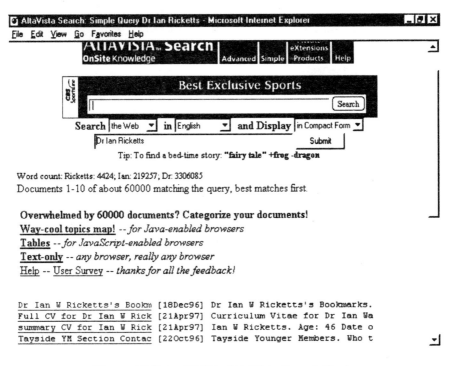

Figure 4.3 Using DEC's AltaVista Search Engine

In this form the WWW would be rather frustrating. It would be like having a telephone connected to the international network but without access to either a telephone book or directory enquiries. How do you find the addresses of the pages which are of interest ? The answer is to use a *Search Engine*. A *Search Engine* appears to a user as a WWW site which typically asks for keywords associated with the topic of interest. The *Search Engine* then replies with a list of links to WWW sites which claim to be offering information on these topics. One of my favourite search engines is *DEC's AltaVista* (www.altavista.dec.com) and figure 4.3 shows an example of its use.

You will find easy access to several popular search engines via the WWW address http://www.computing.dundee.ac.uk/search.html. as shown in Figure 4.4.

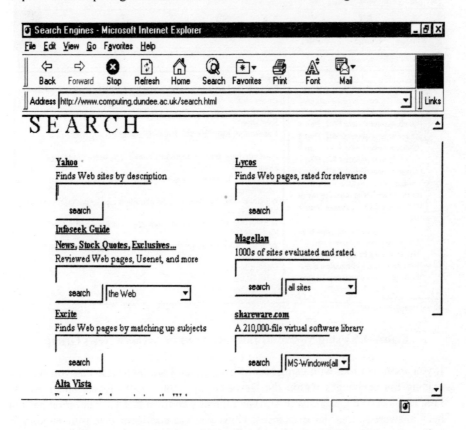

Figure 4.4 Easy Access to Several Popular Search Engines

News Groups

News Groups are another useful source of information. You can consider them to be the Internet equivalent of a notice board. You can post a notice on the board which is then available to be read by anyone else. Any reader can then post their reply either to the notice board or directly to you if you provided your email address in your posting.

I use Microsoft Internet News to access the News Groups from my PC. I have included in Figure 4.5 an example of a typical display when accessing the Artificial Neural Networks News Groups (comp.ai.neural-nets). Your college Information Technology Service will advise you on what News Readers are supported locally and will also be able to offer advice and support in their use.

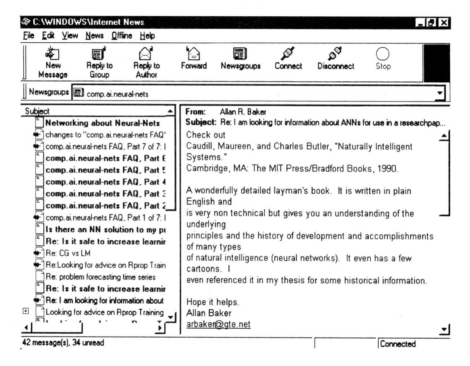

Figure 4.5 Using Microsoft Internet News to Access a News Group

If you are unfamiliar with using News Groups then I would advise that you start by reading the exchanges within the News Group. You should locate and read the Frequently Asked Questions (FAQs) and thereby confirm that your question has not been answered in earlier exchanges. Once you are confident that your enquiry is both appropriate and novel then post it and wait for the response. The speed and high quality of responses makes News Groups an extremely valuable resource but be aware that it is not only experts that you will find on the News Groups.

Do take care when accessing the Internet that you do not offend others by the content of your messages. Consult your Information Technology for guidelines on how to use the Internet responsibly and these will probably be similar to the *Code of Conduct for the Use of Computing Facilities* provided at Dundee (http: // www.dundee.ac.uk / ITServices / codecond.htm). A simple test of content is to ask yourself whether you would be willing to have your message published in your local newspaper together with your name and address. Remember that the News Groups are accessible to millions of Internet users and some of them are journalists and may well live in your home town.

WWW Archives

There are a large number of sites on the Internet which hold software archives and whose contents are freely available for you to download to your computer.

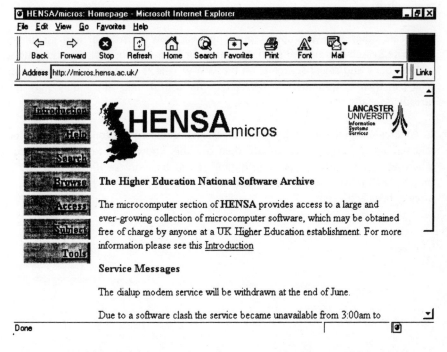

Figure 4.6 Using Microsoft Internet Explorer to Access a WWW Archive

The Higher Education National Software Archive (HENSA), for example, contains software relating to most areas of education but other sites may hold software, articles and data on a particular application area, such as the Genetic Algorithms archive which can be found at http://www.aic.nrl.navy.mil/galist/ or the repository for machine-learning databases at ftp://ics.uci.edu/pub/machine-learning-databases/

Whatever project you are about to embark on, there is a strong possibility that someone else has done something similar and that they have made their work accessible to you via the Internet. Take the time now to locate them via the WWW and read what they have written. You may also be able to download both a copy of their software and their data sets so that you can then see how they achieved their results and perhaps even repeat some of their experiments.

Now when you develop your solution to your customer's problem you will be more confident that it is novel and you can perhaps demonstrate its effectiveness using a data set common to earlier researchers in the field.

Remember to acknowledge those researchers who provided you with the base on which to build and let other researchers know what you have achieved perhaps via a News Group posting. You could even make your report and software available via the WWW so that the next generation of researchers can build on what you accomplish.

To locate other WWW archives open up your WWW Browser and go to your favourite Search Engine and ask it to search for 'archives' or look up your Internet address book and select someone on the WWW who is working in the same field. You can then inspect their WWW pages for useful links since they may have already done the searching for you.

In conclusion, you should assemble a research database by consulting both local and remote resources. You should then use this knowledge to help you decide where to make your unique contribution and to be more confident that you are building on the work of others rather than wasting your effort in repeating what has already been achieved.

5. Selecting the Tools
for Report Production

*One reason humans now rule the animal kingdom
is that we learned to use tools.*

In this section we will examine a number of tools that will help you with the production of your report. However all of them require competence with a keyboard and if you are not already a reasonably competent touch-typist then the start of a project is an excellent time to start acquiring that skill.

Learn to Touch-Type

You can teach yourself to touch-type with 20 x 1 hour lessons using one of the many computer based typing tutors. You will not be up to audio typing by the end of 20 hours training but you will be able to type a lot faster that you can write with a pen. Thus not only will you recover your investment in training time when it comes to producing your final report but you will also save money since you will find it more efficient to produce your own report rather than to call on the services of a secretary.

Once you have learned to touch-type you will reap the rewards each time you use a computer keyboard and since you are at the start of your career as an Information Technologist you will be able to save a considerable amount of time and effort in future.

Using a Word Processor to Write Your Report

I strongly recommend you familiarise yourself with one of the range of word processors that will be available at your college. The skills that you develop will be of use not only in creating your project report but also in creating your curriculum vitae, writing letters for job applications and providing reports and essays for the myriad of courses that you will be following. Your Information Technology advisers, located either within your computing service or within your own department, should be able to recommend a particular software package and advise on its purchase and support its use.

Microsoft Word is one of the more popular word processors within my university and it is currently the word processor of choice within my department. I use it to prepare all my letters, memos, lecture notes, research proposals and articles. Consequently I can exchange documents with my colleagues and call on support whenever I get into difficulty or want to explore a new facility.

I chose Microsoft Word to create this book and we will now examine some of the facilities it provides and which are common to most word processors.

Outlining as an Aid to Report Production

A common problem, met when writing a long document, is deciding the organisation of the information that you wish to communicate. The solution is to use incremental construction also known as outlining. The approach is identical to that used in planning an essay using pen and paper. You start by deciding on a first level heading or working title. You then produce the second level headings as a list of short verb phrases, which provide an expansion of the title. You then expand each second level heading into a number of third level headings and so on, creating a hierarchy of headings, e.g.

Karate - fighting for fitness

Kata - learning the standard defensive moves

Kumite - practising scripted moves with an opponent

Free Fighting - practising unscripted moves with an opponent

Assembling the hierarchy of headings requires you to make some decisions about the length of the final document. If your department provides a guideline for the length of a report, i.e. a maximum page count and suggested headings, then use it. In the absence of such a guideline I suggest you plan for 5 sections totalling 60 pages, as presented in the next chapter, and then discuss and agree your plan with your supervisor.

Once a page count is chosen, I suggest that each section should be 5-15 pages in length (target 10) and that each page should contain from 1-5 headings (target 2) and that you should use a maximum of 4 levels of headings including the title.

You should re-examine the outline as you expand it and modify the order of headings and sub-headings until you are satisfied that the ordering of the outline is optimal (or until you exhaust the time allocated to the activity) and then you can add the paragraphs and sentences relevant to each sub-heading.

The advent of personal computers has seen the introduction of tools to support outlining within the operation of a word processor. As with pen and paper, you can create a list of headings and sub-headings, but the editing facilities of the word processor enable you to re-order the headings until you are content with the structure. You can also insert additional headings and sub-headings as and where you wish.

Once the outline is created you can start to enter the sentences associated with each heading. Unfortunately it is at this stage, when dealing with even quite small documents, that you start to lose track of the intended structure of the document. As the volume of text grows you can no longer see the headings together on the screen and so it becomes difficult to recall the overall structure. However the word processor based outlining tools permit you to selectively hide or display text, at the press of a key. Thus you can easily and quickly switch between full text views and outline to remind yourself of the underlying structure that you had defined. You can also be more selective about which parts of the document are seen in outline and which are not seen.

As an example here are 3 views of the same document as would be seen using the outlining tools. First with just the top level headings visible we see:

1 Introduction

2 Planning for a Project

3 Executing the Project Plan

4 Producing the Report

5 Assembling Your Research Database

6 Managing Your Supervisor

7 Publishing Your Report

8 Managing Stress

Next we have selected to see 3 levels of headings so that we can see more details of the structure:

1 Introduction

2 Planning for a Project

2.1 Identifying the Activities in the Project

Finally we have selected to see all the headings and the included sentences for section 2.4.1

> *You should be able to produce your commented computer program at a rate of 60 lines per day. That is assuming that you have already produced the detailed design and that testing and debugging are separate activities from coding. Assuming that we are planning for a 20-week project, then according to the project time scale given in fig 2.4, coding will be completed in 3 person-weeks or 15 person-days. Therefore you will be able to produce a maximum of 900 lines of source code.*

> *No module should be longer than a page, say 50 lines of source code. Thus the 900 lines of source code will be contained in a minimum of 18 separate modules.*

Using the outlining tool you can choose what is hidden and what is displayed. You can also insert further headings or sentences into your report from within the outlining tool and so expand it, whilst maintaining a clear view of its overall structure.

In common with all tools, you will have to set time aside to learn how to use outlining but once mastered it will repay that initial investment handsomely. Assuming that you are familiar with the basic word processor facilities it should not require more than 2 hours to familiarise yourself with outlining.

Including a Table of Contents

A table of contents gives a concise overview of the structure and content of your report. Assembling the table of contents, until recently, was a task that was embarked on only after the body of the text was completed. This was because assembling the headings with their corresponding page numbers was time consuming and any subsequent changes to the body of the text could force rebuilding of the table of contents. However modern word processors handle the production of a table of contents almost automatically. Typically you need only specify the level to which you want headings included, e.g. first and second level headings, and the format for page numbering of the contents, and the table of contents will be generated at the press of a key and inserted into your document at a position of your choosing.

The ease and speed with which you can assemble a table of contents, combined with the structure of headings and sub-headings provided using the outlining tool means that it is easy to maintain an accurate table of contents throughout the production of the report.

There follows a copy of the table of contents created when I completed an earlier draft of this section of the book. As you can see from an inspection of the page numbers, several of the sections were then present only in outline and the contents of the final book, as can be seen from consulting the final table of contents, contains several major changes.

(Partial) Contents of an Early Draft

Thus you and your supervisor can use the table of contents of your draft report to monitor progress as the page numbers associated with each section grow with each revision.

Including an Index

An index is included to help the reader locate a particular item of information within the report. Its production using current word processors, as with the production of the table of contents, has been largely automated.

To produce an index you must first select all those words and phrases in your report that you wish to be included in the index. Declaration of each entry will typically require a single key press. Then once you have selected all the index entries you move to the section of your report in which you wish to insert the index table using

than a table of values:

Activity	%
Requirements	15%
Design	25%
Code	15%
Test	35%
Report	10%

The problem we wish to solve is how to produce an effective display, i.e. one which enhances the reader's understanding, with the minimum of effort. One means of achieving this is to use a graph tool as an integral part of the word processor that you are using to create the report.

Most graph tools use a tabular form of data entry and then provide a menu to give access to a range of graphical outputs including line charts, pie charts, XY scatter diagrams, plus combinations of each of these components and 3-dimensional versions.

A good graph tool will require you to enter the data once and then permit you to examine the range of possible outputs, with minimal key pressing, until you find an output format which matches your needs. Once you have identified your preferred style of graphical output you can then edit the defaults provided by the graph tool e.g. change fonts, annotate axes, highlight areas of particular interest, before including the final display as part of your document. An integrated graph tool will also enable you to subsequently edit the input data and the format of the output.

As an example, the following graphical displays were produced, in less than 10 minutes, including the data entry, using Microsoft Graph from within the Microsoft Word processor:

	Req.	Design	Code	Test	Report
Bill	3	5	3	7	2
Jane	2	2	5	5	4
Jill	4	3	5	3	6
Tom	5	1	2	1	5

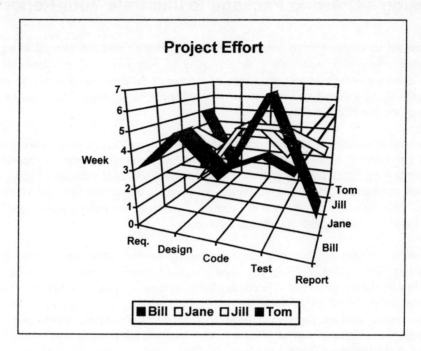

Figure 5.2 A 3-D Graphical Display Created Using Microsoft Graph

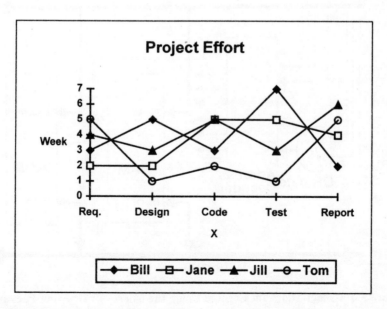

Figure 5.3 A 2-D Graphical Display Created Using Microsoft Graph

Using a Drawing Package to Illustrate Your Report

Now let us examine what support there is for creating and including drawings within your report. Again there are a number of alternative and well integrated software packages available which run on a range of different computers. I do not want to review them here but rather to show what can be achieved with a relatively small amount of effort using them.

A drawing package contains a number of tools to help you create your drawing on its canvas prior to incorporating it into your report. These tools, normally accessed via the mouse, provide you with the ability to create the basic elements of straight lines, curves, text, circles and rectangles. All elements are capable of being selected and once selected can be moved, copied or resized. Several elements can be selected together and then handled as a group.

Once a drawing is created it can subsequently be re-loaded into the drawing package and revised. You can also copy groups of elements from one drawing to help with the production of a similar but different drawing. Once you have invested in assembling a library of basic drawings then illustrating becomes a much faster and simpler activity. Figure 5.4 shows an example of a computer block diagram which was created as part of an examination question but could just as readily be part of the documentation for a report:

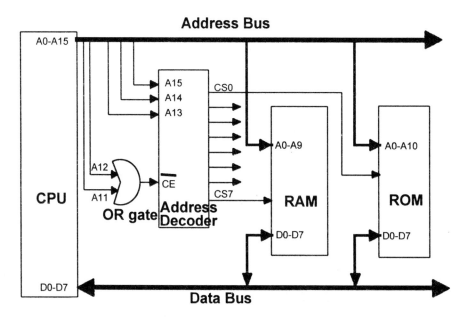

Figure 5.4 A Block Diagram Created Using the Microsoft Drawing Package

The first time you create a drawing like this it will probably take you an hour but thereafter producing a similar drawing will take only a small fraction of that time. Standard libraries of symbols can be purchased to accelerate your production or alternatively, if there are a number of students using the same drawing package, a group of you could create a shared project library.

Including Equations in Your Report

It is quite common to include formulae within a report. Suppose you are required to include multiple integration and summation operators in the formulae, then until recently this would have entailed using a specialist word processor which catered for mathematical symbols. However you can now achieve this using a popular word processor with the addition of an integrated equation editor.

As an example of what is possible the following were produced using the Equation Editor supplied as part of the Microsoft Word processor:

$$\Phi(\alpha,\beta) = \int_0^\alpha \int_0^\beta e^{-(x^2+y^2)}\, dx\, dy$$

An example illustrating the inclusion of matrices into a formula:

$$p(\lambda) = \det(\lambda\, \mathbf{I} - \mathbf{A}) = \begin{vmatrix} \lambda - a_{11} & \lambda - a_{12} \\ \lambda - a_{21} & \lambda - a_{22} \end{vmatrix}$$

and a reasonably complicated example of subscripts and superscripts:

$$erf(z) = \frac{2}{\sqrt{\Pi}} \sum_{n=0}^{\infty} \frac{(-1)^n\, z^{2n+1}}{n!\,(2n+1)}$$

and none of the above took more than 5 minutes of this infrequent user's time to create.

Unlike some equation editors you can see the elements of the equation as you build them - what the cognoscenti call WYSIWYG, pronounced wizzy-wig, and meaning What-You-See-Is-What-You-Get. I would strongly recommend whichever tool you select that you choose one which is WYSIWYG.

6. Writing Your Report

Sales staff are a key part of every successful company.
They are usually very effective communicators and
they receive a large proportion of the top salaries.

Student projects are assessed almost entirely on the written report. Report production should therefore be of prime importance to you. In this chapter we will examine how to create both the structure of your report and its content using a range of tools introduced in the previous chapter.

Creating a Structure for Your Report

What follows is a draft structure for a report and should be used as a basis for discussion with your supervisor. The outcome of those discussions will be an agreed format for your final report. Although production of your report may be one of the last activities to be completed on your project, it is the most important deliverable. I therefore strongly recommend that you start your project by producing an outline structure for the report as it provides an ideal focus for your efforts.

On the assumption that your target is a project report of 60 pages I suggest you use the report structure given in figure 6.1 as the basis for your first outline.

Title

The title of your report is probably one of the last decisions you will make. That is because the title is the ultimate summary of a report and until you have completed the body of your report it is unlikely to be clear what the exact title should be. Prior to the final decision it is normal to work with a provisional title so you can avoid having to admit that you haven't decided what you are doing!

Acknowledgements

This is a short but important section. A number of people usually contribute to a project but by custom the title page only bears the name of the author. The acknowledgements section gives you the opportunity to say thanks to the support team. If you have any difficulty naming them, imagine for a moment that you had to conduct your project on a deserted island but that you can bring along any of the assistants that you name in this section.

Section	Size (pages)
Title	1
Acknowledgements	1
Contents	1
Summary	1
Introduction	15
Method	15
Results	10
Conclusions	8
Recommendations	3
References	1
Bibliography	1
Glossary	2
Index	1
Appendices	
Source code listings	
Test specification	
Detailed results	
Project Plan	

Figure 6.1 Draft structure for your report

Contents

This is a short section which contains a collection of chapter headings and sub-headings gathered together with their associated page numbers. Its purpose is to help the reader to see the structure of the report and to quickly locate a particular section. To avoid too much detail I suggest that you include no more than 4 levels of sub-headings.

You will find one example of a table of contents in the preface to this book.

Summary

This is usually one of the last sections to be written since its completion requires you to produce in 3 or 4 paragraphs a description of the entire project and this is only possible after the body of the report is completed.

Introduction

The introduction is often the last of the main sections to be completed although it is usually the first to be started. In it you will outline the problem whose solution is the focus of your project. Material for this section will be gleaned from the requirements analysis and your review of the literature.

Method

This is likely to be the first main section of the report to be completed since it is a technical description of the method of solution and this is normally the part of the report with which you are most familiar. It also includes the detailed design of the components of the software solution. A decision which you must make is the level of detail which you include in this section and this will be largely determined by the page targets which you agreed earlier.

Assuming that you cannot include all the details of the design of every module in this section then you should include the overall design and perhaps an example of one module's detailed design and then transfer the remaining design details to the appendix and refer the reader to it.

Results

This is another section which is usually completed at an early stage because the reporting of results is a relatively straightforward activity. The challenge with this section is to present the data in a form which is readily absorbed by the reader rather than taking the easier route and presenting the data in the form that was produced by the computer.

We are all familiar with having read, with difficulty, reports containing tables of results, presented to a level of accuracy which was both mind-numbing and probably statistically insupportable. How much more helpful it would have been to see a graphical summary of the results with the detail available to be consulted in an appendix.

The challenge is then to discover what form of presentation is most helpful to the reader. A number of competing presentation formats were introduced in the previous chapter. You will also find many more relevant examples by consulting those project reports already held by your department.

Conclusions

You must remember that the reader does not have your experience of the project and may not appreciate the significance of the results reported in the previous section. It is in this section that you interpret the results for the reader and make it clear what you see as the major outcomes of the project.

Recommendations

Having almost completed the project and accumulated the experience from it, you are now in an ideal position to make recommendations as to areas for further work. It is likely that you can suggest alternative methods of solution which could usefully be investigated e.g. Baker's algorithm should be investigated and its performance compared to that of Able, or alternative means of implementing the solutions, e.g. parallel processing, that would improve the project results, or tools and techniques which would enhance the interpretation of the results e.g. 3-D graphical displays.

You have in this section an opportunity to influence future projects and also to transmit to the reader those ideas which, time permitting, you would have explored.

References

This is a short but important section. It contains an entry for each paper or article to which you referred in the body of the report and sufficient detail in each entry that the reader can obtain their own copy. The reference list is usually numbered or organised alphabetically so that the reader can quickly find a particular entry.

The following are examples of references to a chapter of a book, an article in a journal, a paper given at a conference and a project report:

> (1) **Intelligent Systems for Speech and Language Impaired People: A Portfolio of Research**, AF Newell, JL Arnott, AY Cairns, IW Ricketts, P Gregor, p83-102, Extra-Ordinary Human Computer Interactions, ADN Edwards (Ed), ISBN 0-521-43413-0, Cambridge University Press, 1995.

> (2) **Growth Screening and Urban Deprivation,** E White, A Wilson, SA Greene, W Berry, C McCowan, AY Cairns, IW Ricketts, J Med Screening (1995) 2 140-145.

> (3) **Computer-Assisted Assessment and Management of Patients with Asthma - A Preliminary Report,** C McCowan, RG Neville, AY Cairns, IW Ricketts, FC Warner, RA Clark and GE Thomas, Conference Proceedings Healthcare Computing 1997 Part 1, Pub. BJHC Ltd. Surrey (1997), p117-121, ISBN 0948198265

> (4) **Bilateral Comparison of Breast Images to Detect Abnormalities,** EA Stamatakis, PhD project report, University of Dundee, 1995.

Bibliography

This contains a list of books and articles which, although not essential to understanding your project report, will provide the reader with useful background information. Typically you include here the references to the manuals for whichever operating system and computer language were used on the project. The list might also include a selection of introductory texts to the topic addressed in the project report.

The format of the entries in the bibliography is the same as that used in the reference section but with the addition of a sentence or two explaining why you included the entry.

A bibliography, using the suggested format, is included with this book.

Appendix

The appendix is the report's equivalent of a storage locker. It's a place where you can keep material that you believe is important to the reader's detailed understanding of the project but which is not required in the main body of the report.

Alternatively, an appendix enables you to restrict the main body of the report to the absolute minimum necessary for the reader to understand the project achievements.

Typical entries in the appendix include:

Source Code Listings

This is a copy of all the source code for the project. All modules will contain explanatory comments.

Test Specifications

All the information that a reader would require to repeat the white box tests and thereby verify the correct performance of the project software.

Detailed Results

The complete data set from which was compiled the graphical summaries presented in the results section of the main body of the report.

Project Plan

The last version of the project plan that shows the effort actually expended on each phase together with the actual dates on which the deliverables were produced. This is a valuable piece of the project's history and will be of considerable use when planning for future projects.

Project Meeting Reports

The brief one or two page reports which you write at the conclusion of each project meeting can usefully be included in the appendix. They give the reader of the project report a very useful insight into the project's progress and how you managed the inevitable problems which arose.

Diskette

You should include a diskette with your project report that contains the following computer readable files held in sub-directories:

- a 'readme' file explaining the contents of the diskette (held in the **root** directory)

- the complete project report (held in the **report** sub-directory)

- the source language version of the project code (held in the **source** sub-directory)

- a command file that will build an executable version of the project code (also held in the **source** sub-directory)

- executable versions of all program(s) (held in the **bin** sub-directory)

- all test data (held in the **testdata** sub-directory)

- all results (held in the **results** sub-directory)

The information on this diskette will provide a valuable resource for future projects and can also provide the basis for publicising the project via your department's WWW site or similar Internet access point.

You may want to use one of the file compression utilities to reduce the volume of files that you keep on disk. These utilities typically reduce your files to 10% of their original size and when required you can recover the original file contents without any loss of information. Copies of these utilities are readily obtained via the WWW archives introduced in chapter 4.

Glossary

A glossary is a small dictionary. It contains an alphabetically ordered list of the technical terms that you used in your project report together with a brief explanation. It is included as a separate section so that readers unfamiliar with terms can find the meaning intended by the author, and so that readers who are familiar with the terms are not interrupted by unnecessary explanations in the main body of the project report.

By including a glossary you are also demonstrating that you are aware of the varied needs of readers and that you wish to support them. However you have limited time and insufficient space to include 'A Complete Dictionary for Software Projects' so you will need to be selective.

You can consult the glossary, included with this book, for an example of one possible format.

Index

An index is a partial list of the topics contained within the report, arranged in alphabetical order, together with the page number(s) on which the topics can be found. It is included to help the reader find a particular item of information whose location may not be obvious from an inspection of the table of contents, e.g.

A

Agenda for a project meeting · 82
Alcohol · 23

C

Coding · 68, 87
Contents · XI
Coping with stress · 21
Curriculum Vitae · 85

D

Debugging · 72, 87
Deliverables · 10
Detailed design · 65
Developing your project skills · 15

An index can be compiled, semi-automatically, using the tools provided with most word processors, as explained in the previous chapter.

Strategies to Improve Your Writing

Use a Just-Do-It Approach for Short Reports

Asked to write a short report, of say half a page in length, I usually do not create a written plan but rather I remember the four or five ideas that I want to communicate and just write a first draft. I leave it for a few minutes and then I re-read it and revise it. Depending on the content I use this *just-do-it* approach for writing a document up to a page in length but above that length I find that the time I spend revising the draft versions increases rapidly until I reach a point where I fail to complete them.

Use a Top-Down Approach for Longer Reports

On a good day I might manage to create a three page document with the *just-do-it* approach but more likely I'll get *writer's block*. Then I'll sit staring at the empty page unable to start writing. I'll either have no ideas, or have too many and be unable to separate them long enough to commit them to paper. This is a very frustrating activity so I try to avoid it and if I fail to avoid it I try to recognise it as quickly as possible and stop.

To create a longer document I use a different approach. I subdivide the writing task until it becomes manageable. I break down the original single task into a series of smaller and therefore easier tasks, each of which culminates in the production of a sub-document. I make a note of what ideas each sub-document must convey and confirm that the overall flow of ideas is what I want to achieve. You could call this a document production plan. These smaller documents, none of which will exceed 1 page in length, I then create using the *just-do-it* approach.

The *top-down* approach to producing a project report is to take the first level outline, i.e. the set of chapter headings, perhaps based on the advice in the previous section, together with their estimated page count e.g.

> Introduction (15 pages)
> Method (15 pages)
> Results (10 pages)
> Conclusions (8 pages)
> Recommendations (3 pages)

You should then subdivide each chapter by identifying a series of component headings and sub-headings together with an estimate of their associated page count until you have broken down each document into components whose size you can confidently handle using the *just-do-it* approach.

An introductory chapter on Share Price Prediction might be subdivided into:

> An Introduction to Share Price Prediction (15 pages)
>> Explain the Problem (3 pages)
>> Give a Critical Assessment of Previous Work (8 pages)
>> Suggest Where Useful Work Remains to be Done (4 pages)

Which might then be further subdivided into:

> An Introduction Share Price Prediction (15 pages)
>> Explain the Problem (3 pages)
>>> Role of Stock Market and Trading (1 page)
>>> Random v Non-random Events (1 page)
>>> Potential Value of a Successful Predictor (1 page)
>> Give a Critical Assessment of Previous Work (8 pages)
>>> Prediction in General (4 pages)
>>>> Weather Forecasts (1 page)
>>>> Poker (1 page)
>>>> Horse Racing (1 page)
>>>> Life Expectancy (1 page)
>>> Share Price Prediction (4 pages)
>>>> Futures Market (1 page)
>>>> Currency Market (1 page)
>>>> Metal Market (1 page)
>>>> Gold Market (1 page)
>> Suggest Where Useful Work Remains to be Done (4 pages)
>>> Using Emerging Technologies (3 pages)
>>>> Artificial Neural Networks (1 page)
>>>> Fuzzy Logic (1 page)
>>>> Genetic Algorithms (1 page)
>>> A Combined Strategy (1 page)

The task of writing a chapter of 15 pages has now been reduced to one of writing 15 separate 1-page sections each focused on a single topic. Assuming we are familiar with each of the topics this should be readily achieved using the *just-do-it* approach.

An Approach to Overcoming Writer's Block

Some writers experience little difficulty in producing well structured sections which convey useful information, look attractive and are easy to read. The rest of us have to work somewhat harder to achieve the same results.

When I find myself with a blank sheet of paper and a lack of flowing sentences with which to fill it, a condition some call *writer's block*, I treat the blank sheet like a clean blackboard. I write down any topics or sub-headings that seem relevant anywhere on its surface. The position of topics on the page does not matter at this stage in the process. In this first cycle I don't think long and hard, I just write what comes to mind and keep writing until the flow stops. Then I read over the phrases and write down any further topics prompted by re-reading until the flow stops again. Now I take another blank sheet of paper and re-write the topics in what seems to be a logical order and if further topics come to mind I insert them as the structure develops.

Depending on the size of the task I may repeat the structured re-writing phase two or three times. Usually I expect to arrive at a reasonably well structured set of topics or ideas within twenty minutes of starting. If I am taking significantly longer then I put down my pen and take a ten minute break. A walk to the coffee machine is often all that is needed. Then I start again. If I find that *writer's block* is still in my way I put the writing task to one side and apply my effort to something different and do not return to it until after a break of a least an hour.

Let's suppose I had to write 6 pages on how to organise an inshore sailing trip, then using the above approach I would first produce a page of relevant topics (the following was produced in 14 minutes):

How to Organise an Inshore Sailing Trip

weather forecast	route	crew
inshore forecast	load GPS way-points	who is free
satellite photo	check maps	personalities
food	craft	tide times
what will folk eat	whose boat is available	high tides
what is quick & easy	how many crew needed	
menu		
alcohol	ports	equipment list
lager & real beer	overnight harbours	sails & ropes
whisky & gin	adequate shelter	flares

white & red wines	bad weather stops	life raft & jackets
some liqueurs		water & gas
time plan	book a date	coast guard
pre-departure	pick a date	register trip
shopping	confirm crew	

Then after a 5 minute break I would produce the draft of a structured outline:

How to Organise an Inshore Sailing Trip

1   **Identify Possible Date(s) for the Trip**

2   **Confirm Availability of Vessel**
2.1   Bill's boat (6 berth)?
2.2   Mary's boat (4 berth)?

3   **Select Route (dependent on vessel location)**
3.1   Confirm maps on board and up to latest revisions
3.2   Check pilot for overnight stops
3.3   Confirm emergency shelter points
3.4   Check times of tides for departure & arrival
3.5   Load way-points into Global Position System (GPS) Navigator

4   **Organise Crew**
4.1   Who can co-exist
4.2   Who is available

5   **Plan Food and Drink**
5.1   Food
     5.1.1   What will people eat (and is quick and easy)
     5.1.2   Compile a list of emergency rations
     5.1.3   Assemble a menu
5.2   Alcohol
     5.2.1   Estimate requirements for lager & beer
     5.2.2   Estimate requirements for whisky & gin
     5.2.3   Estimate requirements for white & red wine

6   **Pre-Departure**
6.1   Buy the food and drink

7   **Pre-Sail Check**
7.1   Confirm long term weather forecast OK
7.2   Confirm short term inshore forecast OK

     7.3   Get latest satellite picture

8   Departure Check List
     8.1   Sails & ropes
     8.2   Flares
     8.3   Life raft & life jackets
     8.4   Water, diesel & cooking gas
     8.5   Medical cabinet
     8.6   Register trip with Coast Guard

Assembling the above structured outline took a further 20 minutes using the outline tool supplied with Microsoft Word. The detail is finer than for a project report since none of the first level headings would expand to more than a page and therefore the second level headings are not essential. However having them would ease the writing task.

The final stage would be writing the sentences to describe each of the headings.

Helping the Busy Reader

You should assume that the reader is a busy person who is unlikely to have the time to read your report from beginning to end. It is much more likely that they will read a subset of chapters. Therefore if you are to maximise their understanding you must structure your report to enable the reader to start reading and understanding at almost any point in the text.

To achieve this you should use a hierarchy of summaries throughout the report:

- The title of the report is the highest level of summary.

- The chapter titles are the next level of summary and should succinctly describe the contents of each chapter.

- At the start of each chapter you should include an introductory paragraph describing the content of the chapter and at the end of each chapter provide a paragraph to remind the reader of the chapter's content and its connection to the following chapter.

- Within each chapter the headings should be chosen so that they summarise the content of the relevant section.

This chapter introduced a potential structure for your report including target page counts. It also contained several strategies to assist you in writing the text to fill the structure including the *just-do-it approach* for short reports and the *top-down approach* for longer reports. Finally the chapter closed with a section on overcoming writer's block.

Now, with all other aspects of managing a software project having been dealt with, the next chapter will address the remaining topic of software development.

7. Developing the Software

"I built that", she said with more than a hint of satisfaction.

The software development process consists of a sequence of activities which are performed repeatedly until the software produced meets the customer's requirements or until someone turns out the lights. If you manage your project effectively then the former outcome is the more likely.

In this chapter we will examine each of the activities involved in one cycle of the software development process, from capturing the customer's statement of requirements through to the user's acceptance of the final program. The management decision as to how many times you repeat the software development cycle, will depend on your individual project. It will be one of the many decisions that you will make, with support from your supervisor, when you assemble your project plan and which you will probably need to modify in the light of experience.

We will now examine each activity in the software development process.

Creating the Statement of Requirements

The project starts with a Statement of Requirements. Ideally this is produced by the user. Typically it is a single page description of what the user believes they need. Some users are willing to discuss their requirements at length but are not willing to take the 20 minutes necessary to produce the written Statement of Requirements. If your users are in this class then assist them by preparing the document, preferably as your discussions progress, and then ask them to approve what you have both prepared by signing off:

Approved as an accurate and full Statement of Requirements

signed _____   *date* _____

The Statement of Requirements forms the basis for the next stage of the project. It is also another component of your final project report.

Example Statement of Requirements

StockWatch was a 130 hour project completed by competing teams of six students over a period of five weeks. The aim of the *"StockWatch* project was to develop a program for a local company of stockbrokers in Dundee, that would continuously monitor Stock Market share prices and inform the broker when any of the shares exceeded specified limits. The project included production of the requirements, design, prototypes and final program and also all the relevant testing and documentation".

One team produced the following statement of requirements after an initial one hour meeting with the client and completing some background reading on the topic:

Functional Requirements

Initial Requirements:

1. *The user should be able to select shares to monitor using a price trigger.*
2. *All incoming data should be checked against the user's criteria.*
3. *The user should be informed when any criteria are met, by continuously displaying relevant information until the user acknowledges receipt.*
4. *All alerts and warnings of criteria reached should be written to a log file along with the time an alert was initiated.*
5. *The user should be provided with a comprehensive Help System.*
6. *Enable the user to evaluate stocks using Relative Strength Index values.*
7. *The system should be tolerant of a 'market crash'.*
8. *The system should support multiple users.*
9. *The user should be able to turn off the alert system.*

Advanced Requirements:

1. *Enable the user to check and view seasonal price fluctuations.*
2. *Allow the user to analyse specific stocks which may fluctuate seasonally.*
3. *Inform a user when a stock appears to fluctuate seasonally.*
4. *Provide the user with relevant seasonal information.*
5. *Inform the user of trends i.e. any stocks dropping significantly.*
6. *Enable the user to analyse specific market areas e.g. Oil, Electrical, Banks, etc.*
7. *Enable the user to calculate and perform checks on moving averages.*
8. *Enable the user to view historic share price information.*

Non-Functional Requirements
1. *The software should run on a 386/486 PC with 4 megabytes of RAM.*
2. *Assume the resolution of the client's monitors to be 640x480 pixels.*
3. *The software should extract data from the Reuters' live market feed.*
4. *The program should run under the Microsoft Windows v3.1 operating system.*
5. *The program should interface with Microsoft Excel v5.*
6. *....*

Delivery Requirements
1. *The final software, together with relevant manuals and documentation should be available for presentation on Friday of week 5.*
2. *A first prototype of the software and the requirements should be available on Tuesday of week 2.*
3. *A second prototype to be available for presentation on Thursday of week 3.*

The complete *StockWatch* statement of requirements was two pages in length.

Analysing the Statement of Requirements and Writing the Requirements Specification

This is the next stage where you examine the statement of requirements and produce a more detailed explanation of the requirements. The purpose of this stage is to anticipate the detailed questions that will need to be answered when you start to think of possible solutions.

Suppose that part of the statement of requirements says:

> 'You are requested to design and construct a remote control handset for an electrically operated garage door. You will be responsible for all electronics and associated packaging. The receiver for the messages transmitted by the handset will be sited above the centre of the garage door. .... '.

Then during the requirements analysis phase you might seek answers to the following questions from the user:

*   What is the maximum operating distance required for the transmitter ?

*   Will the door be in sight ?

*   Does the device need to be battery driven?

- Is there a maximum size and weight for the device?

- Does it require to be waterproof ?

- Will it require to be operated in the dark ?

- Can we assume that the operator will have a normal range of physical skills ?

- Do the communications between transmitter and receiver need to be secure?

- etc.

Try to avoid thinking of *how* you will solve the problem but rather concentrate on exactly *what* is the problem.

Example Requirements Specification

The *StockWatch* team produced the following requirements specification based on expanding their statement of requirements as given earlier.

1. The user should be able to select shares to monitor using a price trigger.
The user should be able to monitor the price of selected shares using a price trigger, which will inform them when the selected shares reach a predefined value. Firstly the user must select a share that they wish to monitor by entering the company's symbol. After a share has been selected the user can then input the criterion that the share must meet before an alert is triggered. The criterion for a stock or share will be either a buy or sell price. The system will then monitor all the incoming values from Reuters looking for all company share prices which meet the criterion.

1.1 Select a share
The user will select which shares are to be monitored by entering the relevant company symbol.

Rationale: All companies are represented on the stock exchange by their company symbols. If it is necessary to search a spreadsheet for a company's data then the most efficient way to do this is using the company symbol.

1.2 Input share criterion
The information required to be entered .....

The *ShareWatch* requirements specification was four pages long and addressed each of the nine initial requirements.

Rapid Prototype to Confirm the Requirements

A rapid prototype is a piece of software developed to provide the user with a (partial) view of the eventual system. It is the software equivalent of the hardware designer's polystyrene model that is used to demonstrate the 'look and feel' of a system. Just as it is understood that the polystyrene model will not form part of the final system it must also be understood that the rapid prototype will ultimately be discarded. Given that the prototype will be discarded then the normal procedures of quality assurance associated with software development, such as detailed design and extensive testing, can be omitted.

In the case of the *StockWatch* project the team used Microsoft's Visual Basic to quickly assemble a prototype program which showed one possible format for the User Interface including access to the functions defined in the requirements specification. Then they presented the prototype to the client, together with the requirements specification. This gave the client the opportunity to confirm the requirements:

> To verify that the list of functions was complete

> To provide feedback on the layout of the interface

> To establish confidence in the project team's ability to solve the problem

Rapid prototypes tend to have a 'string and sealing wax' construction but they are still surprisingly effective at providing a channel for communication between the developer and the user. You ignore their potential at your peril.

Remember that your prototype does not have to be software. You can achieve similar results by providing your client with paper drawings of an interface plus explanations of what happens, 'when that button is pressed the display changes to (present next drawing), and if you then select ...'

Several of the competing teams working on the *StockWatch* problem used Microsoft's Powerpoint slide presentation software, instead of Visual Basic, to create their prototype. They used Powerpoint's drawing tools to assemble a slide on the computer screen illustrating the layout of their user interface and simulated the effect of button presses, 'and if you pressed here', by switching between the various slides. Powerpoint makes a very effective tool for rapid prototyping.

You will have completed the requirements analysis phase when you have user approval that your requirement specification is accurate and complete. The simplest mechanism to confirm this is to include the following on the front cover of your document:

Approved by the user as an accurate and complete Requirement Specification

signed _____   *date* _____

The *ShareWatch* team's requirements specification was approved, subject to minor amendments, in the subsequent meeting with the client.

In summary, you capture and document your user's requirements and then support this with a rapid prototype to demonstrate what you understand to be the required functions. Fortified by your user's evaluation you are now in a position to consider how to design the software to provide the agreed functions.

Alternative Approaches to Requirements Analysis

Those readers who have completed a course in software engineering will have been introduced to one or more of the techniques of structured systems analysis and I would strongly recommend that you apply these techniques to your project since they will provide you with a strong base on which to build your solution.

Readers who are new to structured systems analysis may wish to consult one of the myriad of software engineering textbooks for an introduction to the topic, of which Schach [Schach93] and Sommerville [Sommerville96] are good examples.

There are also a variety of computer based tools to support software development, usually referred to under the title of Computer Aided Software Engineering (CASE), but in what follows I will not assume a knowledge of either systems analysis or CASE tools.

Producing the Detailed Design

Typically the design will be produced using a top-down approach and step-wise refinement. In case you are not familiar with this terminology the following example should help.

Requirement:

Make the breakfast

Design:

Initial Step

Make the breakfast

1st Refinement:

Make the breakfast
  Lay the table
  Make the tea
  Make the toast
  Prepare the cereals
  Boil the eggs

2nd Refinement:

Make the breakfast
  Lay the table
    Take the tablecloth from the drawer
    Take the cutlery from the drawer
    Take the dishes from the cupboard
    Place the tablecloth on the table
    Place the cutlery on the tablecloth
    Place the dishes on the tablecloth
  Make the tea
    Fill the kettle with water
    Switch the kettle to boil
    Put tea in the tea pot
    Wait until the kettle has boiled
    Pour the hot water into the teapot
  Make the toast
    Put bread in the toaster
    Switch on the toaster
    Wait until the toast is cooked

> Butter the cooked toast
> Place the cooked toast in the toast rack
Prepare the cereals
Boil the eggs

The process of refinement is repeated until the description of each step is such that it can be readily translated into a computer language. The statements which make up the detailed design are referred to as the Program Design Language (PDL). Using simple English language statements for the PDL has the advantage that it is widely understood. Once the PDL is translated into the computer language, i.e. coded, the program will only be understood by those people who have learned that language. In particular the user's involvement in the development process will cease until the user acceptance stage.

In the last refinement of the design there will be approximately one PDL statement for each line of source code. Thus, using the software productivity estimates suggested earlier, for the 20-week project there will be a maximum of 900 lines of PDL to be produced.

Reviewing the Design

You should review your software designs to ensure both that individually they do what you proposed and also that collectively they meet the requirements that you have agreed with your client.

A review can take several different forms. The simplest and least effective is where you inspect your own designs to identify any errors that they may contain. It is ineffective because, as with many things, we seldom recognise our own errors. A more effective approach is to present your designs to one or more technically qualified listeners and to describe what each module was supposed to do and then to take the reviewers through the details of the program logic that you have assembled. The most effective form of review starts with you circulating your designs to a panel of technically qualified reviewers. At a subsequent meeting, the reviewers provide a number of different combinations of input values, chosen as being those most likely to cause difficulty for your program. Your task is to explain how your design will process the input values.

As with most things, the best results usually require the greatest investment. However remind yourself that errors detected in the earlier phases of software development are far cheaper to repair than errors detected in the later phases. An error in the specification phase which remains undetected until the user acceptance phase is likely to require much more work in re-design, re-coding and re-testing once it is eventually detected than it would have cost to detect and repair during the original specification phase.

You may be able to organise a review team by gathering together fellow project students with each of you presenting your own work for review by the others. This form of review has several potential benefits. A review by your peers is less traumatic than by your superiors. A peer review also provides you with an opportunity to learn how others deal with design problems without you having to specifically ask for their help. You will also be exposed to examples of good practice which you may choose to adopt.

An alternative to a peer group review is to agree with your supervisor that you will assign one or more of your regular meetings to be design reviews.

In summary, all software phases are likely to have errors in them and the longer the errors remain hidden the greater will be the cost to repair them. Design reviews offer one mechanism for locating faults and you are strongly advised to use the technique in your project. Once a design has been reviewed, revised, reviewed again and ultimately agreed, then the next phase of software development is coding.

Coding

Developing software of a quality that is acceptable to the user is time consuming and consequently an expensive process. It is important therefore that code can be re-used with minimum effort so that you get the maximum return on your investment in its development. To achieve this write your code assuming that it is going to be read by someone unfamiliar with your project. That person could be a future maintainer or a fellow student wanting to build on what you achieved. Your first reader might even be your project examiner! Remember that the source code listings can be included in the appendices to your report and it is on the basis of reading and understanding these listings that the examiner will determine a mark to reflect your coding skills. It pays to write code that can be easily read.

You should read at least one of the text books on software engineering for detailed advice on how to improve the quality of your code and how to raise its potential for re-use. Some simple suggestions are that you enhance the readability of your code by using meaningful variable names and that you include explanatory comments throughout the source code. You should also include a descriptive header at the beginning of each source code module. A possible format for the header is:

Module: root.c

Version: 2.0

Author: Ian W Ricketts

Purpose: This module calculates the roots of a quadratic equation.

Inputs/Outputs/Side-effects:

Inputs: 3 real values: x_squared_coeff, x_coeff and konstant
Outputs: 2 complex values: root_1 and root_2.
Side-effects: The global 'success' flag is reset on entry to the routine
and set on exit if the result is successfully produced.

Revision History:

V2.0 / iwr / 1 June 1997
  Root finding algorithm replaced with AB Seas Foolproof method
V1.1 / iwr / 15 May 1997
  Design altered to make the code easier to understand
V1.0 / iwr / 1 January 1997
  Original version

To Compile: cc -O3 -o root root.c

Remember to keep the revision history up to date. Maintaining this level of information in the source code will make it less likely that you will issue an outdated version of the software and it will also help readers of your source code to see what problems you met and how you resolved them.

Using an Integrated Development Environment

An Integrated Development Environment (IDE) appears to the user as a program which streamlines the development of software. IDEs come in a variety of shapes and sizes. On IBM compatible personal computers examples of IDEs include Microsoft's Visual Basic and C/C++ packages, Borland's Delphi and C/C++ products and Symantec's C/C++ product. Typically they all include a source code editor, an integrated compiler and a source level de-bugging tool.

A Source Code Editor

As a minimum this will enable you to save/load files previously created and offer support for entry and editing of your source code. Additional facilities may include the editor having a knowledge of the syntax of the particular language that you are using and thus the ability to detect the use of incorrect syntax. The editor may also provide automatic formatting of the source code i.e. indenting the text between repetition statements. Once you have entered a section of source code a single command should call the integrated compiler from within the editor.

An Integrated Compiler

This will compile the source code into an executable form. It will detect any syntax errors not previously detected by the source code editor and if any errors are found it should return you to the source code editor with a pointer to the location of the syntax error(s). Compilation of a module will take only a second or two. Once you have completed entering the source code and you have corrected all syntax errors you will then need to confirm that the module meets your requirements. To achieve this you will use the source level debugging tools normally supplied with IDEs.

Source Level Debugging Tools

These provide you with a source code view of your program and permit you to inspect and alter the values assigned to variables within the module and then execute the code, either line by line or in blocks delimited by breakpoints whose location you define. After each phase of execution you can inspect the values of the variables and thereby confirm that the module is functioning as required.

Source code debugging makes it relatively easy to detect errors in your modules and then to locate and remove them. It also provides a powerful tool for testing your source code as outlined in the next section.

Verification & Validation

Verification and validation are the names given to the checking processes which ensure that software conforms to its specification and meets the needs of the user [Sommerville96]. They are two separate activities which are performed throughout the software development process. Verification is checking to confirm that the output from a software development phase meets that phase's input specification. Validation is checking to confirm that the output of a software development phase meets the user's requirements.

Examples of verification are the tests you run on completion of the coding phase to confirm that each module meets its design specification, i.e. you check that the results of the coding phase meet with the requirements of the coding phase as defined by the design specification.

An example of validation is when, at the completion of the coding phase, you re-examine the user's requirement specification to confirm that you have produced the code to meet all their needs.

We will complete this chapter by examining the verification and validation of the source code in more detail.

Testing Individual Source Code Modules

As stated previously, efficient software development requires that in each phase of development you should aim to remove all errors before proceeding to the next phase. Testing source code refers to the four stage process of detecting the presence of errors, i.e. unpredicted outcomes, locating and removing their causes and finally re-testing the module to confirm that the source code is error free.

There are a variety of techniques to help you detect errors in routines for which you have a knowledge of the structure of the code. The so-called glass box or white box techniques include statement, branch and path testing and you will find details of these and other techniques in the classic text by Myers [Myers79]. Alternatively you can consult almost any text on software engineering of which McConnell [McConnell93], Schach [Schach93] and Sommerville [Sommerville96] are good examples.

Branch testing is one way of increasing your confidence that a piece of software does not contain errors. It is not guaranteed to detect all errors but then neither is any other readily applied testing technique.

To develop a branch test you examine the design of a module and identify each possible branch within it. Assuming that a module takes only a single item as input, you choose a range of different values for that item so that it forces the program to follow each and every possible branch at least once. For modules that accept multiple items as input, you select those combinations which activate each branch. You also predict, prior to conducting the test, what the corresponding outputs from the module will be. You then create a test specification for each module which contains, as a minimum, all the pairs of inputs and predicted outputs required to exercise all branches in the module.

Performing the branch test consists of supplying the module with those inputs, examining what output is actually produced and noting, in a test report, the outcomes of each test. The minimum entry for a test report might look like:

Test Report for Module Root.C

Tests performed by IWR on 5/11/93 according to test specification: ROOT.TSP (Version 1.3)

test 1   Passed

test 2   **Failed** - predicted output was 3.41 but actual output was 1.78e56

test 3   Passed

etc.

When errors are detected a further and separate activity is performed which is often referred to as de-bugging. De-bugging is finding the exact cause of an error and removing it. You are then required to repeat all the branch tests on the module to ensure that there are no further errors awaiting detection. These further errors may have been present when testing commenced or introduced when you repaired earlier faults.

Once you have successfully completed the branch testing you can have some confidence that the module contains no (obvious) errors and you have documentary evidence, in the form of test reports, to confirm it.

Testing Your Integrated System

Once you have established that the individual modules all pass their respective module tests then you can combine the modules and check that the integrated system continues to operate correctly. One approach to system integration is the *Big Bang* approach, in which you combine all components in a single step and then test to confirm that the integrated system operates satisfactorily. An alternative approach is *incremental integration* where you combine modules one or two at a time and then check for correct operation. You remove any errors that your tests detect, retest to confirm all detectable errors have been removed and then integrate another one or two modules and retest the combination. The procedure is repeated until all the modules are integrated into a single system and all detected errors have been removed.

The area that you must search to locate errors is much smaller when using incremental integration. However this gain is partially offset by the need to repeat some of the testing with each cycle of the incremental integration. Overall *incremental integration* is usually much faster than the *Big Bang integration,* perhaps because you can assemble most of the *incremental integration* tests by re-using combinations of the individual module tests.

The *StockWatch* share price monitoring system, which is comprised of approximately 3000 lines of source code in 85 modules, was checked using 44 system tests. The test specifications and reports covered 22 pages of the appendix to the final project report. An example of one of the smaller and successful tests follows:

User Input - Test Number 13

This test is designed to check that the data that the user enters for a share note is transferred to the spreadsheet and that this data is correctly recalled when selected in the monitoring program. This test is essentially a manual check and to accomplish it the tester will have to enter a note on the stock within the monitoring program for a particular share and then check the corresponding spreadsheet to see if this note is saved on the sheet. The tester will then need to select a different share in the monitoring program, then re-select the original share and confirm that the note is still available. This test will need to be repeated for each different type of share.

Results from User Input - Test Number 13

During test run 1 the share note was stored in the correct spreadsheet location and recalled correctly when switching through several different shares each with their own share note. However a problem was detected when a company's record was deleted. The information on the company is removed but the note is retained. The remaining companies' records are then moved up to fill the space left by the deleted company record but the note from the deleted company now becomes associated with the company which replaced the deleted record. This error is to be removed.

User Acceptance Testing

Once you are confident that your system is performing satisfactorily, i.e. you have completed the module and incremental system testing, then the next stage is to expose your program to the user. The user's role is to check that their requirements have been met by running a series of tests which may be based on those you created for the system testing phase. You should monitor and if required assist with the tests and note all deficiencies. This phase also provides the user with an opportunity to evaluate the final interface to the program and to make any further suggestions for improvements.

The acceptance test may highlight an error in the requirements specification which will require a complete iteration of the development process to correct. However, you are more likely to locate deficiencies in the design or implementation phases which will only require partial iterations. You should not expect to complete the acceptance testing phase without the user finding some deficiencies. It is therefore common practice to plan for at least two cycles of the software development process.

In conclusion, you start your project by identifying the user's requirements which you then proceed to meet by executing the sequence of activities collectively known as the software development process. This culminates with you presenting your work for assessment by that original user or users to assess how close you have come to meeting their requirements. The software development process is finally completed when the user accepts that the program meets their requirements.

References

1. Software Engineering, by Stephen R Schach,
   Pub. Aksen Associates, 1993, ISBN 0-256-12998-3

2. The Art of Software Testing, by GJ Myers,
   Pub. John Wiley, 1979, ISBN 0-471-04328-1

3. Software Engineering, by Ian Sommerville,
   Pub. Addison-Wesley, 1996, ISBN 0-201-42765-6

4. Code Complete, by Steve McConnell,
   Pub. Microsoft Press, 1993, ISBN 1-55615-484-4

Bibliography

Here are ten good sources of information for any student embarking on the management of their software project.

1. Code Complete, by Steve McConnell,
   Pub. Microsoft Press, 1993, ISBN 1-55615-484-4

   A practitioner's reference book with lots of examples and supporting statistics.

2. Doing Your Research Project, by Judith Bell,
   Pub. Open University, 1995, ISBN 0-355-19094-4

   Although intended for researchers in Education and Social Science, the practical advice in this short book is of much wider relevance.

3. Essential Visual Basic 4.0 *Fast*, by JR Cowell,
   Pub. Springer-Verlag, 1996, ISBN 3-540-19998-5

   Visual Basic is a great tool for prototyping and this is a very good guide to using it.

4. A Guide to Usability, by Jenny Preece,
   Pub. Open University, 1993, ISBN 0-201-62768-X

   A good introduction to usability and its evaluation. If you want to make your software more acceptable to your user then read this short text.

5. Poem for the Day, Edited by Nicholas Albery,
   Pub. The Natural Death Centre, 1995, ISBN 1-85619-499-X

   '...medical research at Bristol University indicates that poetry reading is as good a cure for depression as pills'... so I recommend this for those less than perfect days. It is more portable than television and acts faster and lasts longer than alcohol.

6. Professional Awareness in Software Engineering, Edited by Colin Myers,
   Pub. McGraw Hill, 1995, ISBN 0-07-707837-3

This compilation from the wider aspects of the profession is a refreshing antidote to the often narrow focus of a project.

7. Software Engineering, by Stephen R Schach,
   Pub. Aksen Associates, 1993, ISBN 0-256-12998-3

   An A-Z of software engineering and almost as easily accessed.

8. Software Engineering with Student Project Guidance, by Barbee Teasley Mynatt, Pub. Prentice Hall, 1990, ISBN 0-13-826231-4

   A clear and practical guide to applying software engineering to a student project.

9. Statistics in Practice - an Illustrated Guide to SPSS, by Basant K Puri,
   Pub. Arnold, 1996, ISBN 0-340-66209-3

   If you are in need of a light to shine on the 'black art' of statistics then I recommend you read this short practical guide.

10. The Management of a Research Student Project, by K Howard & JA Sharp,
    Pub. Gower, 1991, ISBN 0-566-00613-8

    This short book is based on the authors' experiences of PhD supervision at Bradford Management Centre and while software engineering is not addressed their advice on research project management provides ample reward to the reader.

Appendices

An Example Statement of Requirements

<u>Gold Price Prediction System</u>

<u>STATEMENT OF REQUIREMENTS</u>

Summary

Explore using an Error Back Propagation Neural Network (EBPNN) to predict the dynamics of gold prices as quoted on the London market.

Outline

- Gold prices (closing, day_high & day_low) are published daily in the Financial Times newspaper (FT). Back copies of the FT are held in the college library from which a price history can be compiled covering the last 5 years.

- Neural Networks are reported as being capable of learning by example and the majority of reports of successful applications used EBPNN.

- Explore training an EBPNN on a subset of the gold price data, say the first 2 years, and test its ability to predict the price changes for the following 2 weeks.

- Explore the usefulness of incorporating additional economic metrics into the prediction model e.g. FT100 index, etc.

  - Investigate the effect on the prediction performance of varying the number of inputs and hidden layers in the EBPNN.

Bibliography

1. Course notes for the 4th year module in Neural Networks which includes an extensive reading list.

2. *Introducing Neural Networks*, Alison Carling, published by Sigma Press, UK, 1992, ISBN 1-85058-174-6.

3. Understanding Neural Networks - Computer Explorations, Maureen Caudhill and Charles Butler, published by MIT Press, USA & UK, 1992, ISBN 0-262-53099-6.

Outline of a Project Plan

'Gold Price Prediction System'

PROJECT PLAN (Version 1.0)

Project Activities		Milestones	
	Duration (week numbers)	Project Deliverables	Week ending number
	0	**Statement of Requirements**	**0**
(Requirements Analysis) Research into gold price variations & neural networks for prediction Compile gold price data	1-3	(Requirement Specification) 1st Draft of Introductory chapter (gold price variations & neural networks for prediction) Data file with 5 years of gold prices	3
Stage 1			
(Design) Produce the design for the Error Back Propagation Neural Network (EBPNN)	4-5	(Design Specification for stage 1) **PDL for EBPNN**	5
(Implementation) Code EBPNN	6	(Implementation Specification and Software Modules - stage 1) **EBPNN module(s)**	6
(Testing) Specify and conduct test on EBPNN module(s)	7-9	(Test Spec. for stage 1) **Test specification for EBPNN**	7
		(Test Reports for stage 1) **Test reports for EBPNN**	9

(Reporting) Prepare project report chapter from specs.	10	(Report for stage 1) **1st draft of chapter on EBPNN design i.e. method chapter**	10
Stage 2			
(Design) Refine design of EBPNN	11-13	(Design Specification - stage 2) **PDL for refined EBPNN**	13
(Implementation) Code refined EBPNN	14-15	(Implementation Specification and Software Modules - stage 2) **refined EBPNN module(s)**	15
(Testing) Specify and conduct test on refined EBPNN module(s)	16-19	Test Specification for stage 2 **Test specification for refined EBPNN module(s)**	16
		(Test Reports for stage 2) **Test reports for refined EBPNN**	19
(Reporting) Complete the project report	20	Report for stage 2 **Draft of completed project report**	20
(Operation & Maintenance)		(User Manual)	

Outline of a Project Report

Gold Price Prediction System - Report Plan (version 1.0)

Section	Size (pages)
(Title) Gold Price Prediction System	1
(Acknowledgements)	1
Contents	1
Summary	1
Introduction	15
Method	15
Results	10
Conclusions	8
Recommendations	3
References	1
Bibliography	1
Glossary	2
Index	1
Appendices	
Source code listings	
Test specification	
Detailed results	
Project Plan	

An Example Agenda for a Project Meeting

<u>Gold Price Prediction Project</u>

MEETING AGENDA

1.   **Progress**

    1.1 Statement of Requirements (2 mins)

    1.2 Requirements Analysis (10 mins)

2.   **Plan**

    2.1 Completion of the Requirements Analysis and Specification (10 mins)

    2.2 Detailed Design for Phase I (20 mins)

3.   **AOB**

    3.1 Lack of adequate access to development computers (2 mins)

    3.2 Upgrade of 'C' language compiler ? (2 mins)

    3.3 School's Liaison demonstration (2 mins)

    ......

4.   **Next Meeting** (2 mins)

An Example Report of a Project Meeting

Gold Price Prediction Project

MEETING REPORT

Time: 2-3pm 29th February 1994 (end of week 2 of the project plan)

Present: Dr A. Einstein + Helm Holtz

1. Progress

1.1 Statement of requirements acceptable once minor amendments made. HH to produce updated document.

Action: HH

1.2 Requirements analysis draft 1 discussed.

page 2 sect 1.1 - explanation unclear - redraft

Action: HH

page 3 sect 1.4 - flow charts would help understanding - redraft

Action: HH

....

2. Plans

Currently proceeding as planned, thus latest plan as produced 21/2/94.

2.1 Complete requirements analysis and production of requirement specification by end of week 3.

2.2 Detailed design for phase 1 scheduled for weeks 4-5.

3. AOB

3.1 Lack of adequate access to development computers

AE will explore at Dept Meeting (3rd March) all staff agreeing to a booking system with projects given priority access outside normal laboratory hours.

Action: AE

3.2 Upgrade of 'C' language compiler ?

Arrange purchase of the software update to version 6.3

Action: AE

3.3 School's Liaison demonstration

HH to set up a demonstration of the 'robot arm' chess game for the visit by the school's liaison panel 2-3pm Tuesday 7th March. Demo to be ready for next project meeting.

Action: HH

4. Next Meeting

Next meeting   2-3pm   6th March in AE's office - AE providing doughnuts!

Action: AE

Meeting finished 2.55pm

Outline of a Curriculum Vitae (CV)

Curriculum Vitae for Joseph Alfonse SOAP

Date of birth: 31 September 1972

Place of birth: Halifax, Yorkshire

Term address: Flat 2a, 23 Hilltop Street, Newtown.

Tel: (3423) 123 1231

Home address: Wuthering Heights, Heckmondwyke, Yorkshire.

Tel: (0643) 453 2322

Period of College Study: October 1994 - June 1998

Qualification Obtained: Honours BSc (Upper Second) in Applied Computing

1st Year Courses (and results)

Introduction to Software Engineering I	65%
Data Structures & Algorithms I	73%
Information Technology I	67%

2nd Year Courses (and results)

Introduction to Software Development II	69%
Data Structures & Algorithms II	70%
Information Technology II	69%

3rd Year Courses (and results)

Graphical User Interface Programming	60%
Human Computer Interaction	63%
Software Engineering I	72%
Software Engineering II	68%
Architecture & Operating Systems	65%
Team Project	67%

4th Year Courses (and results)

Computer Vision	63%
Artificial Intelligence	64%
Programming for the Internet	66%
Business Studies	69%
Project	72%

Title: Neural Networks Applied to Predicting Share prices

Supervised by: Dr A Einstein

Summary: Applied a back-propagation neural network to learning the dynamics of fluctuations in the price of gold on the London market.

Extra Curricula Activities:

Member of the University Swimming Team 1994-1996

Member of the University Rucksack Club 1994-1998

Member of the Public Speaking Society 1994-1998

Student member of the British Computer Society (BCS) 1994-1998

Secretary of the BCS student branch 1996-1997

Glossary

Abstract- this is a very short summary of a longer piece of writing or work. Papers submitted to some journals require to be accompanied by an abstract of 50-100 words. Similarly some conference submissions are assessed solely on the basis of a 200-300 word abstract.

Branch Testing - in a branch test you examine the design of a module and identify each possible branch within it. Assuming that a module takes only a single item as input, you choose a range of different values for that item so that it forces the program to follow each and every possible branch at least once. For modules that accept multiple items as input you select those combinations which activate each branch. You also predict, prior to conducting the test, what the corresponding outputs from the module will be.

Coding - translating a detailed design, perhaps written in a Program Design Language (PDL), into a computer language.

Debugging - is finding the cause of an error and removing it.

Deliverables - are the products of a software activity e.g. the deliverables produced by the coding phase of software development are the software modules and the implementation specifications.

Design Specification - is a description of a piece of software, perhaps written using a Program Design Language, which contains sufficient detail that the design can be readily translated into a particular computer language. *See Coding.*

Glossary - an explanation of technical terms arranged in alphabetical order. It is included as a separate section so that readers unfamiliar with terms can find the meaning intended by the author and so that readers who are familiar with the terms are not interrupted by unnecessary explanations.

Implementation Specification - this is one of the deliverables of the coding phase of software development. It is a document which contains a description of the code.

Internet - this is an international communications network which interconnects computers via telephone wire, microwave and optical fibre links. Most of the world's universities and companies are on the Internet and via it they can exchange electronic mail messages, share software and promote their services.

Project - a piece of work, typically lasting from a few weeks to several months, which is selected to encourage a student to practise and develop the skills which they have been taught.

Rapid Prototype - is a piece of software developed to provide the user with a (partial) view of the eventual system. It is the software equivalent of the hardware designer's polystyrene model that is used to demonstrate the 'look and feel' of a system. Just as it is understood that the polystyrene model will not form part of the final system it must also be understood that the rapid prototype will ultimately be discarded. Given that the prototype will be discarded then the normal procedures of quality assurance associated with software development, such as detailed design and extensive testing, can be omitted.

Requirements Specification - is a detailed description and expansion of the user's needs based on their statement of requirements. It aims to answer all the questions that a software developer will have when designing the solution.

Statement of Requirements - is a brief description, in perhaps 1-2 pages, of the user's needs. *See Requirements Specification.*

Step-Wise Refinement - is a general approach to problem solving in which a problem which is too large to solve, is subdivided into smaller problems which because of their reduced size may now be amenable to solution. If not then the process is repeated. Ultimately the problem will be reduced to a series of sub-problems which are small enough to be solved.

Test Report - is a document which details the outcome of a test including any unexpected results. *See Test Specification.*

Test Specification - this documents, as a minimum, all the pairs of inputs and predicted outputs required to test a module. *See Branch Testing and White Box Testing.*

Time Management - the concept of Time Management is that you divide your working day into hourly slots. You identify what goals you wish to achieve and what series of tasks will need to be completed to reach the goals. You then estimate how much time you will need to complete each task. You can then allocate your time accordingly.

User Manual - is a document that contains all the information that a user requires to operate a software system and which is written in a style that the user can readily understand.

Validation - is confirming that the output of a software development phase meets the user's requirements. *See Requirements Specification.*

Verification - is confirming that the output from a software development phase meets that phase's input specification e.g. confirming that a module of code does/does not contain any errors.

White Box Testing - is a collection of techniques to help detect errors in routines for which we have a knowledge of the structure of the code. The White Box techniques include statement, branch and path testing. *See Branch Testing.*

World Wide Web (WWW) - is an alternative view of the information available on the Internet. You can create a Web Page, containing information that you wish to share, using *Microsoft Front Page* or similar program. You can then make your Web Page accessible to other Internet users by linking your Web Page to a Web Server.

Index

U

T

V

W